WARREN W. WIERSBE

T0339242

MILESTONES
of the MASTER

CRUCIAL EVENTS IN THE LIFE OF JESUS
AND **WHY THEY MATTER SO MUCH**

LEXHAM PRESS

Milestones of the Master:
Crucial Events in the Life of Jesus and Why They Matter So Much
© 2015 by Warren W. Wiersbe

Lexham Press, 1313 Commercial St., Bellingham, WA 98225
LexhamPress.com

First edition by Weaver Book Company.

Print ISBN 9781683591788
Digital ISBN 9781683591795

Cover design: Frank Gutbrod
Interior design: { In a Word } www.inawordbooks.com

Contents

Preface

When I was about to leave for seminary in 1948, my Uncle Simon Carlson, a retired pastor, brought me a dozen books from his library, among them a copy of G. Campbell Morgan's *The Crises of the Christ*. At that time I didn't know who G. Campbell Morgan was, but my reading of that book greatly helped to shape me and my ministry.

In his book, Campbell Morgan discusses seven "crises" in our Lord's earthly career: His birth, baptism, temptation, transfiguration, crucifixion, resurrection, and ascension. The book was published in 1903 at a time when "new theologies" were beginning to infiltrate Christian schools and churches. In his book, Morgan not only answered the liberals of his day but he also met some of the challenges that we meet today.

In his spoken and written ministry, Campbell Morgan exalted Jesus Christ and made God's truth practical and exciting. *The Crises of the Christ* gives us a beautiful example of Bible teaching that encourages us to search the Scriptures and relate one text to another. I'm glad I read the book early in my training because it helped me to love the Scriptures more and to receive the word of God as a treasury of living truth and not as a seminary textbook.

The idea for this present book came from my exposure to *The Crises of the Christ*. During more than sixty years of both pastoral preaching and conference and seminary teaching, I have occasionally given messages on what Morgan called "The Crises of the Christ." I didn't use his title or plagiarize his material, and I always told the congregations where the idea for the series originated. However, in my own series I have added three studies: Jesus in the temple as a boy, our Lord's triumphal entry into Jerusalem, and the sending of the Holy Spirit.

I never met G. Campbell Morgan personally; but in 1970, while ministering in Birmingham, Alabama, I did meet one of his four pastor-sons, Kingsley John Morgan. He was very gracious to spend time with me, and after our conversation he sent me back to my hotel with a bag of books out of his own library. (Shades of Uncle Simon!) Among them were hard-to-find reports of the Mundesley Bible Conference that his father had founded and conducted each summer, plus a stack of his father's individually printed sermons. What treasures!

I have many of Dr. Morgan's books in my library, and occasionally I read a sermon or a chapter to enrich my own soul. I also have a cassette recording of his sermon on Genesis 1:1–2, so I can actually listen to him speak when I have an hour to spare.

I encourage you to secure a copy of Morgan's *The Crises of the Christ* and to study it carefully. It will help you learn more about Jesus and will also encourage you to magnify Him in your life and service. I trust that the book you are reading now will also help you to grow in grace and in the knowledge of the Son of God. Our Lord has a master plan for each of His children and we must not fail to follow it.

Warren W. Wiersbe

Introduction

A Life Planned in Heaven

From the time Jesus was conceived in Mary's womb to His ascension to heaven, everything He did, said, and experienced while He was on earth had been planned beforehand by the Godhead, before the creation of the heavens and the earth. Jesus said, "I do not seek My own will but the will of the Father who sent Me" (John 5:30). He also said, "I always do those things that please Him" (John 8:29). He knew He was under orders and He always obeyed. Jesus rose early each morning and spent time praying to the Father and receiving His "orders of the day" (Isa. 50:4–5; see Mark 1:35). This is a good example for all Christians to follow. In our Lord's earthly life and ministry, there were no accidents, only divine appointments; and so it will be with His obedient people today. "The steps of a good man are ordered by the Lord, and He delights in his way" (Ps. 37:23).

God governs His creation by decree, and not by committee vote or popular consensus. John the apostle heard the multitudes shout, "Allelujah! For the Lord God Omnipotent reigns!" (Rev. 19:6). The Lord says, "My counsel shall stand, and I will do all My pleasure" (Isa. 46:10). King Nebuchadnezzar said of the Lord, "He does according to His will in the army of heaven and among the inhabitants of the earth. No one can restrain His hand or say to Him, 'What have You done?'" (Dan. 4:35). Whether we like it or not, the Lord operates by executive fiat and answers to nobody for what He does.

"The counsel of the Lord stands forever, the plans of His heart to all generations" (Ps. 33:11). The Lord is sovereign and that settles it. But note that His counsel comes from His heart. The will of God is motivated by the love of God and is always well-suited and perfectly adapted to each of His children. He "works all things according to the counsel of His will" (Eph. 1:11). If that were not true, He could never have inspired Paul to write Romans 8:28: "And we know that all things work together for good to those who love God, to those who are called according to His purpose."

Everything that transpired in the life and ministry of Jesus on earth was ordained before the foundation of the world. As you read the Gospel of John, you find that Jesus lived by a divine timetable. At the wedding feast, He said to His mother, "My hour has not yet come" (2:4). When His unbelieving foster brothers urged Him to go to the feast in Jerusalem, He replied, "My time has not yet come, but your time is always ready" (John 7:6; and see vv. 8 and 30). At His last Passover feast, Jesus knew that the time had come for Him to die (John 12:23, 27; 13:1; 16:32), and in His high priestly prayer, He said, "Father, the hour is come. Glorify Your Son that Your Son may glorify You" (17:1). Because Jesus followed God's timetable, He was not afraid of those who wanted to kill Him but boldly kept ministering the word of God. He could say with David, and so may we, "My times are in Your hand" (Ps. 31:15).

I recall the dark day when the seminary registrar called me into his office to inform me that I would have to spend one more year at school before I could graduate. For some reason, he could not accept all the hours I had transferred from Indiana University, so I would actually be spending an extra year to earn my degree. It also meant that my fiancé and I would have to postpone our marriage until after I graduated. (She was on a four-year course.) We could arrange to see each other occasionally, but

I was pastoring a church as well as attending classes, and that was keeping me very busy. As it turned out, she arrived home and found a job waiting for her, and the extra classes I had to attend were exactly what I needed for my ministry! Yes, we had to be patient until my graduation, but as I said, we did see each other occasionally that year. Our times were in God's hands and everything worked out beautifully, as it always does when the Lord is in control.

We can think of successful people in the Bible who learned to put their times into God's capable hands. Abraham and Sarah schemed to get a son before God was ready and they paid dearly for it. Joseph could not understand why things seemed to go wrong in Egypt, but the Lord made him second ruler of the land at just the right time. By rescuing his family from the famine, Joseph rescued the future nation of Israel. Moses tried to use his sword to deliver his people from Egyptian bondage, but his attempt failed and he had to flee. Forty years later, God sent him back to Egypt, and this time the Jewish slaves were delivered. Our Lord's disciples did not always understand what He was doing, but one thing they did know: He was doing the Father's will.

As I look back on more than sixty years of ministry, I can affirm that the Master has a perfect plan for every believer and that He will unfold that plan a step at a time as we obediently follow Him. The purpose of this book is to introduce you to the milestones in the life of Jesus so that you might better understand how our loving God teaches us and guides us today.

The Incarnation and Birth of Jesus

Matthew 1–2; Luke 1–2

From eternity past, the Lord Jesus Christ existed with the Father and the Spirit; and together they conceived what we call "the plan of salvation." The pre-existence of Christ is one of the basic doctrines of the Christian faith. John opens his Gospel with, "In the beginning was the Word, and the Word was with God, and the Word was God. He was in the beginning with God" (1:1–2). Our Lord did not hesitate to say that He came down from heaven (3:13; 6:38, 42, 62; 8:14, 42; 16:28; 17:5, 8). He told Pilate that He had both been born (the physical) and had come into the world (the eternal—John 18:37). Babies are conceived in this world so they don't "come into the world" but only out of the mother's womb. Jesus was miraculously conceived in Mary's womb and in that way came into the world from heaven.

First, the Lord created a universe—the heavens and the earth. Of all the planets God created, He chose the earth to be the stage on which He would demonstrate His grace. "The earth is the Lord's, and all its fullness" (Ps. 24:1). In the creation process, God *formed* and then He *filled*. He formed the heavens and filled them with various lights and galaxies. The land and the seas He filled with vegetation and various kinds of creatures. He climaxed His creative work by making a man and a woman and commanding them to be fruitful and multiply.

As every Bible reader knows, our first parents disobeyed the Lord and brought sin and death into the world. But the Lord gave them the promise of a Redeemer: "And I will put enmity between you [the serpent] and the woman, and between your seed and her Seed; He shall bruise your head, and you shall bruise His heel" (Gen. 3:15). Eventually, God called Abraham and Sarah to found the nation of Israel that would give the world the promised Redeemer. "Salvation is of the Jews" (John 4:22). Abraham and Sarah became the parents of Isaac, and Isaac and Rebekah became the parents of Jacob. It was Jacob who fathered the twelve sons who became the founders of the twelve tribes of Israel.

From generation to generation, the Lord revealed His plans to His people in types and prophecies. Before he died, Jacob told his sons, "The scepter shall not depart from Judah, nor a lawgiver from between his feet, until Shiloh comes; and to Him shall be the obedience of the people" (Gen. 49:10). He was speaking of Jesus, the Son of God.

Some critics wonder why God was so strict with His people Israel during those formative centuries, but we must remember that Israel was called to reveal God to the Gentiles and to bring God's Son into the world. Whenever Israel went after idols and abandoned the Lord, they were jeopardizing that wonderful plan of salvation.

God had chosen a nation, and from that nation He chose one tribe—the tribe of Judah. On his deathbed, Jacob predicted that the promised Redeemer would come from the tribe of Judah (Gen. 40:10). Centuries later, God told David the Savior would come from his family (2 Sam. 7). The prophet Micah announced that the Redeemer would be born in Bethlehem, the city of David (5:2), and Isaiah predicted the Redeemer would be born of a virgin (7:14).

According to Scripture, there are four ways to get a human body. God made Adam from the dust of the earth, and He made Eve from a part of Adam's body. Their sons received their bodies as has every human being since that time, through the union of a man and a woman. *But Jesus received His body through the woman without the man!* Those who deny the virgin birth of Christ are also denying the inspiration of the Scriptures, the deity of Christ, His sinlessness, and His humanity. The virgin birth of Jesus was the first milestone in the ministry of the Savior.

Whenever the Lord wants to get something done in this world, He can speak the word (Ps. 33:9), send angels (Heb. 1:14), or enlist believers who will obey Romans 12:1–2 and give Him their body, mind, and will and obey His commands. But to accomplish the greatest work of all, the salvation of lost sinners, God sent His Son to earth to be a servant. Jesus needed a body to accomplish God's will, and He said to His Father, "Sacrifice and offering You did not desire, but a body you have prepared for Me. . . . Behold, I have come . . . to do Your will, O God" (Heb. 10:5–8). Jesus had to take to Himself a body for at least five reasons.

To Bring Eternal Life to a Spiritually Dead World

Jesus needed a body *so He could bring eternal life to a spiritually dead world.* When Jesus came to earth, "the life was manifested, and we have seen, and bear witness, and declare to you that eternal life which was with the Father and was manifested to us" (1 John 1:2). Zacharias, father of John the Baptist, said it perfectly when he called Jesus "the Dayspring from on high" (Luke 1:78). The world was in mental, moral, and spiritual darkness, and God sent "the light of the world" (John 8:12) to bring the dawning of a new day. People who were "dead in trespasses and sins" (Eph. 2:1) and walking and sitting in darkness (Isa. 9:6; Luke 1:79) could now behold the light of life and experience salvation. The world was controlled by illusion, but Jesus brought reality and demonstrated what life really is. Jesus said, "I have come that they may have life, and that they may have it more abundantly" (John 10:10).

To Die for the Sins of the World

Our Lord needed a human body *so He could die on the cross for the sins of the world.* "And we have seen and testify, that the Father has sent the Son as the Savior of the world" (1 John 4:14). The angel Gabriel made this very clear to Joseph. "And she [Mary] will bring forth a Son, and you shall call His name Jesus, for He will save His people from their sins" (Matt. 1:21). On the night Jesus was born, the angel announced to the shepherds, "Do not be afraid, for behold, I bring you good tidings of great joy which will be to all people. For there is born to you this day in the city of David a Savior, who is Christ the Lord" (Luke 2:10–11). During the many centuries of the old covenant, great numbers of birds and animals were sacrificed on the altar at the Jewish sanctuary, but the blood of those sacrifices could never take away sin. Jesus gave Himself as one sacrifice forever and settled the sin question forever. John the Baptist pointed to Jesus and said, "Behold! The Lamb of God who takes away the sin of the world!" (John 1:29).

To Defeat the Devil and Give Us Victory

Our Lord needed a human body *so that, in His death, resurrection, and ascension, He would defeat the devil and enable us to live victoriously.* "He who sins is of the devil, for the devil has sinned from the beginning. For this purpose the Son of God was manifest, that He might destroy the works of the devil" (1 John 3:8). At His birth and in His subsequent ministry, Jesus invaded Satan's territory, because "the whole world is under the sway of the wicked one" (1 John 5:19).

Luke 11:14–23 is very applicable here. Jesus had cast out a demon and His enemies accused Him of doing so in the power of the devil. Jesus exposed how illogical their reasoning was and then explained that He was stronger than the devil and had stripped him of his weapons and defeated him. "Now is the judgment of this world," said Jesus, "now the ruler of this world shall be cast out" (John 12:31). "Having disarmed principalities and powers, He made a public spectacle of them, triumphing over them in it [the cross]" (Col. 2:15). Satan is a liar, but we have God's truth. Satan is a murderer, but we share God's life. Satan commands the demons, but we are empowered by the Holy Spirit. Satan is the prince of darkness, but we walk in the light of the Lord.

To Show the Love of God

Our Lord needed a human body *so that He might manifest the love of God in His life and ministry.* "He who does not love does not know God, for God is love. In this the love of God was manifested toward us, that God has sent His only begotten Son into the world, that we might live through Him" (1 John 4:8–9). "But God demonstrates His own love toward us, that while we were still sinners, Christ died for us" (Rom. 5:8). People saw God's love in His teaching, His healing of people, His concern and care for the needy, and His suffering and death.

But it isn't enough that we know God's love and through the Holy Spirit experience it. We must also grow in our love for the Lord, for His people, and for the lost. "But the fruit of the Spirit is love" (Gal. 5:22). He wants His love to be "perfected among us" (1 John 4:17). Our Christian love must be perfected because immature love can be selfish love. "And this I pray," Paul wrote to the Philippian believers, "that your love may abound still more and more in knowledge and all discernment" (1:9). Christian love is not blind! As we grow in God's word, we will experience maturing love (1 John 2:5) through the ministry of the Spirit (1 John 4:12–13); and as we fellowship and serve with the saints, our love will grow more and more (1 John 4:16–19).

To Become Our High Priest and Advocate

Our Lord needed a human body *so that He could experience what we experience and become our High Priest and Advocate.* When our Lord returned to heaven, He took with Him a glorified body that had experienced birth, growth, toil, weariness, hunger and thirst, pain, and death. "For we do not have a High Priest who cannot sympathize with our weaknesses, but was in all points tempted as we are, yet without sin" (Heb. 4:15).

"My little children, these things I write to you, that you may not sin. And if anyone sins, we have an Advocate with the Father, Jesus Christ the righteous" (1 John 2:1). The word "Advocate" is the same as "Comforter," referring to the Holy Spirit (John 14:16, 26; 15:26; 16:7). It means "one called to your side to help you" and in the Greek courts referred to a lawyer. Every child of God has the Spirit of God within as a Helper and the Son of God in heaven as a Helper. But please don't imagine that, when we sin, the Father wants to punish us but the Son intercedes and the Father changes His mind. The Father and the Son and the Holy Spirit always work together for our good and for their glory.

Because we have an Advocate in heaven, we can approach Him at the throne of grace, confess our sins, and receive forgiveness (1 John 1:8–10). Our High Priest and Advocate in heaven knows how we feel when we are falsely accused, ridiculed, lied about, disappointed, in pain, grieving the death of a loved one, facing temptation, or any of a myriad of trials that life brings to us, *and He can give us victory!* If we fail, He can forgive us and give us a new beginning. The Lord is not only *with* us, but He is also *for* us. "If God is for us, who can be against us?" (Rom. 8:31).

* * *

Jesus needed a body so He could accomplish the Father's will, and God commands every believer to yield his or her body to Him because He wants to work in us, for us, and through us (Rom. 12:1–2). If we feel weak, our High Priest can give us grace; if we fail, He can forgive us and give us a new start. The Scottish preacher Alexander Whyte used to say that the victorious Christian life is a series of new beginnings, and it is; and each new beginning brings us new strength and new opportunities to grow and serve.

In His incarnation, Jesus laid aside the independent use of His divine attributes and yielded Himself totally to the will of the Father and the working of the Holy Spirit. Paul summarizes this remarkable event in Philippians 2:5–8:

> Let this mind be in you which was also in Christ Jesus, who, being in the form of God, did not consider it robbery to be equal with God, but made Himself of no reputation, taking the form of a servant, and coming in the likeness of men. And being found in appearance as a man, He humbled Himself and became obedient to the point of death, even the death of the cross.

Paul makes it clear that what Jesus did was wholly an act of grace. "For you know the grace of our Lord Jesus Christ, that though He was rich, for your sakes He became poor, that you through His poverty might become rich" (2 Cor. 8:9). Jesus came to earth a human and not an angel. His human body was permanent and today is glorified in heaven and still bears the marks of His crucifixion. He came a baby and not an adult and grew up "in wisdom and stature, and in favor with God and men" (Luke 2:52). He came a Jew, not a Gentile, for "salvation is of the Jews" (John 4:22). He came in humility and became a servant, ministering to men, women, and children by healing them, feeding the hungry, raising the dead, teaching the seekers, forgiving sins, and finally dying for a lost world on a Roman cross.

In the Philippian letter, Paul makes a personal application of the passage quoted above: "work out your own salvation with fear and trembling" (v. 12). We are to be servants of the Lord and lay aside everything that would hinder us from having an effective ministry. Later in that chapter, Paul mentions Timothy and Epaphroditus as good examples of humble servants of God and His people. God is looking for servants and not celebrities or "control freaks." God works through incarnation, not imitation of the world, "for it is God who works in you both to will and to do for His good pleasure" (Phil. 2:12).

Over many years of itinerant ministry, I have met many humble believers who served people sacrificially, but I have also met some who were dictators and expected everybody to serve them. Jesus is our example and He was a servant. "Let this mind [attitude] be in you which was also in Christ Jesus" (Phil. 2:5). Jesus told His disciples, "I am among you as the One who serves" (Luke 22:27). Let's follow His example.

* * *

There are two important elements involved in the birth of Jesus and that should be emphasized today, but they seem to have been forgotten. The first is *joy that a Savior has been given.* During the Advent season, we see and experience excitement and gladness for one reason or another—family reunions, vacations from school, giving and receiving gifts, special foods, traditional music—all of which we are free to enjoy. But where is the joy that we should know because a Savior has been born? And where is the burning desire in our hearts that this message be sent around the world? The first word the angel Gabriel said to Mary was,

"Rejoice" (Luke 1:28), and Mary sang of the joy that was in her spirit (Luke 1:47). When Mary visited Elizabeth, who was pregnant with John the Baptist, the baby leaped for joy in his mother's womb (Luke 1:44). The angel told the shepherds, "Do not be afraid, for I bring you good tidings of great joy which shall be to all people. For there is born to you this day in the city of David a Savior, who is Christ the Lord" (Luke 2:10–11). If the true meaning of Christmas doesn't give us joy, something is wrong.

Advent activities often consume so much time, money, and energy that it's no wonder people complain instead of rejoice. A friend said to me one day, "I wish Christmas didn't come at a time of year when the stores are so crowded." It's difficult to listen to the popular secular holiday music; and in spite of the "Jesus is the reason for the season" banners, our Savior is ignored. But in spite of the competitive and commercial atmosphere, we as God's people can still rejoice *and let that joy be known!* Let's take a positive approach and urge others to share love and joy and spread the good news of salvation.

The second element that often seems to be missing is *giving thanks to God for the gift of the Savior.* In my opinion, our Lord's incarnation is the greatest expression of giving found anywhere in human history. "For you know the grace of our Lord Jesus Christ, that though He was rich, yet for your sakes He became poor, that you through His poverty might become rich" (2 Cor. 8:9). Yes, the wealthy and prestigious magi (wise men) visited Jesus and gave Him valuable gifts, but months before they arrived, the poor shepherds hurried to Bethlehem to see God's wonderful gift and then made it widely known that the promised Savior had been born (Luke 2:17). Let's follow their example. We should think not only of the greatness and glory of God, but also about the needs of others around us. "Let each of you look out not only for his own interests, but also for the interests of others" (Phil. 2:4).

Years ago I preached a sermon which I called "The Magnetism of the Manger." The baby in the manger drew the angels down from heaven to praise Jesus. He also drew the shepherds in from the fields to worship Him and then go out and witness about Him. He drew the magi from distant lands to bring Him gifts and carry the good news to the Gentiles. Today He draws many families and friends together for worship and fellowship. But Jesus Christ is no longer a baby in a manger. He is the exalted Son of God, gloriously enthroned with the Father in heaven, and He deserves our best gifts, our faithful service, and our most devoted worship and witness. May we join Mary in her testimony: "He who is mighty has done great things for me, and holy is His name" (Luke 1:49).

Perhaps the most familiar and beloved Christmas verse outside the four Gospels is Isaiah 9:6: "For unto us a Child is born [His humanity], unto us a Son is given [His deity]; and the government will be upon His shoulder. And His name will be called Wonderful, Counselor, Mighty God, Everlasting Father, Prince of Peace." This prophecy will be fulfilled when Jesus returns and establishes His kingdom, but we can enjoy the blessings of these names today as we make Jesus the Lord of our lives.

Wonderful—This takes care of *the dullness of life.* How many people today are bored with life even when celebrating the birth of the Savior. Counselors tell us that there are people who feel so empty and useless during the holiday season that they attempt to take their lives, and some of them succeed. As Christians, we know that our God is a God who does wonders (Ps. 77:14) and that He opens our eyes to the wonders around us every day.

Some people try to solve the problem of dullness by spending time and money on novelties, changes in geography, or just plain entertainment; but these "remedies" only make the malady worse. Only Jesus Christ can transform life into something wonderful!

He was wonderful in His birth, His life, His death, and His resurrection. He is wonderful in His teaching, His example, His love, and the power He can give us for our daily lives. How anyone could belong to Jesus Christ and be bored with life is a mystery to me. Walking with Jesus is an experience filled with wonder.

Counselor—This takes care of *the decisions of life.* "You will guide me with Your counsel, and afterward receive me to glory" (Ps. 73:24). During my daily devotional time, when I pray for our family, I ask the Father to help everybody make wise decisions and claim James 1:5: "If any of you lacks wisdom, let him ask of God, who gives to all liberally and without reproach, and it will be given to him."

I have counseled many believers in trouble who got there by rushing ahead of the Lord, or delaying obedience, or not seeking His will at all. How my wife and I thank the Lord for His guiding hand and loving heart! We can receive guidance from meditating on the Scriptures, praying, seeking counsel from mature Christians, and giving God time to share His plans with us. The strict translation of the Greek of John 7:17 is, "If anyone is willing to do His will, he will know concerning the teaching." The will of God is not a matter of options or opinions but obligations. If I am not willing to obey, the Lord is not obligated to guide me. "They [Israel] soon forgot His works; they waited not for His counsel" (Ps. 106:13).

Mighty God—This takes care of *the demands of life.* Mary said it best: "For He who is mighty has done great things for me, and holy is His name" (Luke 1:49). Jesus said that "with God all things are possible" (Matt. 19:26). How can we claim to believe the Bible and yet question the ability of our Lord to accomplish great things? The one thing that limits God is our unbelief. "Now He could do no mighty work there . . . because of their unbelief" (Mark 6:5–6). When we have the inner conviction of the Holy

Spirit and confidence in God's promises (Rom. 8:26–28), we may pray with freedom and expect the Lord to act. Salvation is not something God begins and we finish in our own strength, "for it is God who works in you both to will and to do for His good pleasure" (Phil. 2:13). By faith we receive the power of the Holy Spirit (Acts 1:8), and the Spirit enlightens us as to what we should do, empowers us to do it, and enables us to finish His work to the glory of God.

Everlasting Father—How can God the Son also be God the Father? He is not, of course, nor should the text be interpreted that way. The Jewish people use the word "father" to mean "originator of" or "creator." Jesus called Satan "the father of lies" (John 8:44), meaning that lies originated with him. To paraphrase this title, we might say "through God the eternal Son everything originated." When Jesus Christ was conceived in Mary's womb, time and eternity met. When Jesus suffered and died on the cross, time and eternity met, for the Son's great work of redemption was "foreordained before the foundation of the world" (1 Peter 1:20). When sinners repent and trust the Savior, time and eternity meet as they receive the gift of eternal life (John 3:16). In John 7, our Lord's half-brothers ridiculed Him for not rushing to the feast in Jerusalem where He could get back the crowd that had deserted Him (John 6:66). "My time has not yet come," Jesus told them, "but your time is always ready" (John 7:6). We learned in the first chapter of this book that, in His earthly ministry, Jesus lived on a divine timetable that had been ordained from eternity. *But His unconverted half-brothers had nothing eternal in their lives, nor do unconverted sinners today.* God has put in every heart a hunger for the eternal (Eccl. 3:11), but a lost sinner doesn't receive eternal life until he or she trusts the Savior. Then there is a new dimension to their lives, for they are drawing upon the resources of heaven (John 3:27), laying up treasures in heaven (Matt. 6:19–21), and anticipating rewards when they reach heaven. We used to sing a chorus at Youth for Christ rallies that expresses this truth:

> With eternity's values in view, Lord,
> With eternity's values in view;
> Let me do each day's work for Jesus,
> With eternity's values in view.

As we seek to know and do the will of God, we can say to the unsaved crowd as did Jesus, "Your time is always ready." Our times are in God's hands (Ps. 31:15). We live in an exciting heavenly dimension, the dimension of eternity!

Prince of Peace—This takes care of *the disturbances of life.* "Peace I leave with you," Jesus said to His disciples, "My *peace* I give to you; not as the world gives do I give to you. Let not your heart be troubled, neither let it be afraid" (John 14:27—emphasis mine).

The apostles had lived with Jesus for almost three years and they had many opportunities to observe Him, and they never once saw Him worried, upset, afraid, or perplexed. During a fierce storm on the Sea of Galilee, Jesus was asleep in the back of the boat. When an angry mob threatened to attack Him, He simply walked through the mob and went His way. When the temple guards came into Gethsemane to arrest Him, He stepped forward and surrendered so He could protect the disciples. He personified Isaiah 26:3, "You will keep him in perfect peace, whose mind is stayed on You, because he trusts in you." Godly character and God's peace go together. "The work of righteousness will be peace, and the effect of righteousness, quietness and assurance forever" (Isa. 32:17).

In Philippians 4:6–9, Paul gives us the perfect formula for inner peace: right praying (vv. 6–7), right thinking (v. 8), and right living (v. 9). The world gives a counterfeit peace by distraction—watch TV, go on a cruise, throw a party, take a sleeping pill—but the Lord puts the peace in our hearts that enables us to enjoy calmness in the midst of chaos. When I find myself upset, I reach for my Bible and let the Lord calm me down. "These things I have spoken to you that in Me you might have peace," said Jesus. "In the world you will have tribulation; but be of good cheer, I have overcome the world" (John 16:33). "I will hear what God the Lord will speak, for He will speak peace" (Ps. 85:8).

But keep in mind that God gives us peace, not that we might settle back and become spectators, but that we might move ahead and accomplish the work God wants us to do. The peace of God enables us to do the will of God to the glory of God. The Lord may not stop the storms around us, but He can calm the storms within us and, as He did for Peter, enable us to walk on the water.

> The Lord bless you and keep you;
> The Lord make His face shine upon you,
> and be gracious to you;
> The Lord lift up His countenance upon you,
> And give you peace.
>
> —Numbers 6:24–26

(*The Milestone Mirror: A Pause for Reflection*)

Have you ever considered that your birth is important in God's plan? David makes it clear in Psalm 139:13–18 that we were fashioned by God because He has a specific place for us to fill and an important work for us to accomplish. We may never have our photograph on the cover of *Time* or be interviewed on television, but every Christian is important in the eyes of the Lord. Have you accepted this fact and are you praying that the Lord will help you obey?

Are you ever guilty of feeling sorry for yourself because you aren't like other people you admire? If so, confess that sin and start thanking God for how He has blessed you. Settle it now that God put you here, God wants you here, and He will work everything together for good if you will trust and obey (Rom. 8:28). You are so important that Jesus died for you!

Moses argued with God that he was not equipped to lead the nation of Israel, but the Lord asked, "What is that in your hand?" (Exod. 4:2). It was a simple rod, but God used that rod in remarkable ways in the next forty years. What have you in your hand? Give all that you are and have to God and see what He can do!

2

The Boy Jesus in the Temple

Luke 2:39–52

Dr. Luke has told us about the miraculous conception and birth of Jesus Christ and His presentation in the temple in Jerusalem. Joseph and Mary returned to Nazareth with Jesus and "the Child grew and became strong in spirit, filled with wisdom; and the grace of God was upon Him" (Luke 2:40). Twelve years pass between verses 40 and 41, and Dr. Luke tells us nothing about our Lord's childhood years in Galilee. Then he gives us this fascinating account of Mary, Joseph, and Jesus going to Jerusalem to celebrate Passover.

Jewish men were required to go to Jerusalem three times a year to observe the most important of the seven annual feasts (Deut. 16:16). A Jewish boy became a "son of the covenant" at his *bar mitzvah* at age thirteen, but some parents took their sons to Passover in Jerusalem when the boys were only twelve. This gave them first-hand experience of this historic annual feast and helped prepare them for their upcoming *bar mitzvah*. At age twelve they were to get acquainted with the law and from age thirteen on they were expected to obey it.

Families and neighborhoods usually traveled together to Passover in Jerusalem, the women and children in front, setting the pace, and the men following, carrying baggage and keeping watch over the company. The pilgrims might sing the "Songs of Ascents" (Psalms 120–134) as they made this festive journey to the holy city. Journeying to Jerusalem must have been exciting for young Jesus who was about to enter His adolescent years. In childhood, the emphasis is on *investigation,* asking questions, taking things apart, and learning what they mean; but in adolescence, the emphasis is on *integration,* putting things together and finding out who we are and where we belong.

Leaving home and traveling would expose Jesus to new experiences that would contribute richly to his maturing. Dr. Luke tells us that "Jesus increased in wisdom and stature and in favor with God and men" (2:52). His life and personality were balanced, and the eighteen "hidden years" in Nazareth helped to prepare Him for the three busy years of ministry that would culminate in His death, resurrection, and ascension.

A number of practical spiritual truths are found in our Lord's second visit to the temple.

Change

On the journey to Jerusalem, Jesus was facing *the challenge of change.* After being sheltered somewhat in Nazareth, He was stepping out into the big world and confronting things He had heard about but had never experienced.

The way you and I deal with change and freedom helps to determine our character and conduct. It has well been said that, in this life, growing old is *a given,* but growing up is *a personal choice;* and some people make the wrong choices and never find true maturity and freedom. They become either tyrants or wimps.

Christians are supposed to be childlike but not childish. I knew a man who, when a child, deliberately failed third grade because in fourth grade he would have to write with ink. He was not unlike the people who feign illnesses or handicaps so they can escape adult responsibilities. Of course, they are only robbing themselves.

With its fertile green hills watered by bountiful rivers and springs, Galilee was called by some "the fairest region in the land of Israel." In Jesus' day, there were more than two hundred villages and towns in Galilee, and Nazareth was definitely not a "hick town." The region was surrounded by a Gentile population, including Samaria, Phoenicia, and Decapolis, and was called (sometimes in derision) "Galilee of the Gentiles" (Isa. 9:1–2; Matt. 4:15). At least five of Christ's apostles came from Galilee: the four fishermen—Peter, Andrew, James, and John—and Nathanael (John 21:2). The citizens of Galilee had a strong accent that was ridiculed by some Jews (Mark 14:70), and the city of Nazareth, where Jesus grew up, was especially despised. "Can anything good come out of Nazareth?" asked Nathanael, who himself was from Cana in Galilee (John 1:46).

Groups of Galileans arriving in Judea might invite scorn, for in Judea the Jewish religion was strictly observed, while in Galilee (with its Gentile influence) the law was occasionally given a more liberal interpretation. And, of course, Judea had some right to be proud, for Judah was the royal tribe from which Messiah would come (Gen. 49:10) and the tribe could boast of having the city of Jerusalem and the temple of the Lord.

I remember the first time I visited Chicago, which was less than an hour's drive from our home in Indiana. It was during the Christmas season and one of our neighbors was taking his young son to "the city" (as we called Chicago) and invited me to go along. I was speechless with awe when I saw the tall buildings, the congested traffic, the stores with their crowds of shoppers, displays of tempting merchandise, and striking holiday decorations. Years later when my ministry took me to New York City, London, Mexico City, Toronto, and a host of other large cities, the "little boy" in me showed up again whether it was Christmas season or not. I married a farm girl from a small town, but I will always be a city boy.

Jesus must have been deeply impressed with the sights, sounds, and activities in that great city, and most of all in the temple; for when the Galilean pilgrims left for home, He stayed behind in the temple. The building and its activities was unlike the synagogue back in Nazareth, yet He felt right at home, for this was His Father's house. Jesus was opening His mind and heart to a whole new world. There are some Christians who are so satisfied in their own little kingdoms that they do not experience growth from the challenges that come with change.

Freedom

In this event we see *a focus on freedom*. Jesus did not disobey Mary and Joseph when He stayed behind in the temple, for they were wisely allowing Him the freedom to travel with His friends in other groups, and they simply assumed He was with them. Jesus was not a twelve-year-old rebel; He was a twelve-year-old pilgrim, slowly moving toward freedom. He needed that freedom because He was the servant of the Lord who would die for the sins of the world. Jesus lived on God's timetable. The day would come eighteen years later when Jesus would leave Nazareth and journey to the Jordan River to be baptized by John. He would call together a band of twelve apostles to share in His itinerant ministry of preaching and healing.

But at age twelve, He was under the authority of Joseph and Mary, and like all maturing adolescents, He gradually moved into freedom and was occasionally misunderstood. Though He was

God in human flesh, Jesus still had to learn, to grow, and to develop His life skills just as we do today. Hebrews 5:8 tells us that "though He was a Son, yet He learned obedience by the things which He suffered." He went through the developmental stages that every human must experience to reach maturity, and because He did, He fully understands what we experience day by day and can give us grace to overcome (Heb. 4:14–16).

Over the years, I have counseled numerous frustrated teenagers and have asked them, "You say you want freedom. What is freedom?" The usual answer is, "Freedom is the right to do what I want to do, with nobody interfering." But that is not freedom; it's the worst kind of bondage! *Freedom is life controlled by truth and motivated by love.* "And you shall know the truth," said Jesus, "and the truth shall make you free. . . . Therefore if the Son makes you free, you shall be free indeed" (John 8:32, 36). If I have deception or hatred in my heart, I am a slave to sin; but if I am walking in love and in the truth, I will enjoy freedom in Christ. Truth and love must go together, for truth without love is brutality and love without truth is hypocrisy (Eph. 4:15).

When children reach early adolescence, parents need to start "lengthening the cords" and trusting their teens with a little more freedom as they see fit. At one period in our home, our four children were all teenagers! But my wife and I can sincerely say that, as we gradually gave them more freedom, they were cooperative and dependable. (We did a lot of praying!) Our two sons and two daughters had been committed to the Lord even before they were born, and the Lord was faithful to protect and direct them. They knew that freedom was not a vacation from values and virtues but an opportunity to become what God wanted them to become and do what He wanted them to do.

Tradition

Balancing the focus on freedom is *the thrill of tradition,* for true freedom is a dynamic interplay of the old and the new. We cannot live in the past *but we must not prevent the past from living in us.* What would life be like if everybody in the United States lost the past? We would have to call our nation the United States of Amnesia! Imagine having to begin each day re-learning our names, the alphabet, numbers and words, and how to drive a car or use a microwave; yet some members of the younger generation insist that we destroy the biblical and historical traditions of the church.

Joseph and Mary believed in obeying the Lord and honoring the past. They took twelve-year-old Jesus to the ancient city of Jerusalem to participate in an ancient event that belonged only to the ancient Jewish nation. Sharing in the Passover feast in the city of Jerusalem, young Jesus would be exposed to both the history and theology He had heard about in His home and in the synagogue. It's unfortunate that some young people today have rejected valuable traditions that would enrich their lives, accepting instead the cheap novelties that are starving them spiritually. I suspect that more than one Christian teenager comes away from contemporary church services saying, "There's got to be something better than this."

Jesus spent time with the spiritual leaders in the temple, asking and answering questions and amazing them with what He said. Here we have the young and the old interacting with each other and learning from each other. In His life and teaching, Jesus did not reject tradition but built upon it. "Do not think that I came to destroy the Law or the Prophets," He said. "I did not come to destroy but to fulfill" (Matt. 5:17). The late Dr. Jaroslav Pelikan said, "Tradition is the living faith of the dead; traditionalism is the dead faith of the living." Read that again and remember it. The Holy Spirit must be permitted to breathe life repeatedly into our spiritual activities. If not, our churches will become beautiful corpses instead of active living bodies. We will hear the Lord say, "I know your works, that you have a name that you are alive, but you are dead" (Rev. 3:1).

"There is a cemetery next to our sanctuary," said a discouraged pastor, "and I'm discovering that it also runs right through the church!" One cause for the "deadness" of churches is the unwillingness of adults and young people to communicate with each other. Unlike Jesus, the young people may not be asking the right questions, or perhaps the adults are not lovingly listening and giving the right answers. Philosopher George Santayana wrote, "Those who cannot remember the past are condemned to repeat it." I might add that some older folks who think they *are* remembering the past may be confused, for "the good old days" (as I have said before) are often the product of a bad memory and a good imagination.

Jesus was in the temple because it was His Father's house and He was responsible to be about His Father's business. Note that He used the word "must." Years later when He was in active public ministry, He said, "I must preach the kingdom of God" (Luke 4:43) and "I must suffer" (9:22). "And as Moses lifted up the serpent in the wilderness, even so must the Son of Man be lifted up" (John 3:14). *If we want the privilege of freedom, we must accept the responsibility of obedience.* When our teenage children graduated from the driver's training class, they were permitted to apply for their driver's license and have the privilege of driving on the streets and highways. Respect and responsibility go hand in hand in the Christian life. Jesus had respect for the elders and the elders had respect for Jesus, though they did not know who He was.

Tradition is what helps hold society together, whether nations, states, cities, political parties, schools, churches, or football teams and their fans. It's the golden link between generations that helps the older generation prepare the younger generation for one day assuming adult responsibilities, as Paul wrote to Timothy: "And the things you have heard me say in the presence of many witnesses entrust to reliable people who will also be qualified to teach others" (2 Tim. 2:2 TNIV).

Every church is one generation short of extinction. Our English word "tradition" comes from the Latin and means "to hand over." I used to recommend to my ministerial students that they plan a "Heritage Sunday" for their congregations each autumn so they could review the background of the church, the names of key people, and what the Lord had done over the years. Previous generations worked hard and made sacrifices to build and maintain the facilities and ministries that later generations might be prone to criticize. When adult church leaders keep their hands on everything and fail to pass along ministry responsibilities and privileges to the younger generation, the church often becomes stagnant, then dormant, and then silent.

No matter what our ages, our spiritual gifts, or our ministries, we must always be about our Father's business, even if it means forsaking other things (Matt. 19:29). Being the husband of Mary, Joseph was our Lord's legal father; but at age twelve, Jesus announced that His allegiance was first to His Father in heaven. At the wedding in Cana, Jesus made it clear that his mother was not in charge of His ministry (John 2:1–12); and in Mark 3:31–35, He said that His mother and brothers had no special authority over Him. (Joseph was probably dead by then.) When Jesus was dying on the cross, He commanded John to care for His mother and told Mary to go home with His beloved disciple (John 19:25–27), and they obeyed. I like Mary's words to the servants at the wedding in Cana: "Whatever He says to you, do it" (John 2:5). That's good counsel for every believer today.

Submission

We close our study by considering *the satisfaction of submission*. Joseph, Mary, and Jesus returned to Nazareth and Jesus lived there for the next eighteen years until He entered His public ministry. Dr. Luke informs us that Jesus was "subject to them" (Luke 2:51), which most likely includes not only His obedience as a son but also His learning Joseph's trade of carpentry. People called Jesus "the carpenter's son" (Matt. 13:55) and "the carpenter" (Mark 6:3). It's probable that Joseph died while Jesus was still living at home and was prepared to take over the business. Jesus would be called "rabbi" (teacher) and the rabbis each had a trade. They did not accept money from their students but earned their own way.

Once again we see Jesus as an obedient maturing son. "And Jesus increased in wisdom and stature, and in favor with God and men" (Luke 2:52). His growth was balanced—intellectually, physically, socially, and spiritually (v. 52, and see v. 40). When you read our Lord's teachings in the four Gospels, you can see how much He must have learned by observing everyday activities. Yes, He was taught by the Father (Isa. 50:4–6), but God uses many different tools to teach us.

Did He ask about seeds and soils when the farmers brought their plows to be repaired or sharpened? Did He ever help his mother find a lost coin in the house? Did a rebellious neighbor boy ever leave home, waste everything, and then return home and be welcomed and forgiven? Did He personally know any tax collectors? When He heard the Scriptures read in the synagogue Sabbath service and in the children's class, did He penetrate its meaning? What about the Passover lamb, or the uplifted serpent (John 3:14–15), or Isaac on the altar (Gen. 22)? Did He ever watch his mother put yeast in the bread dough?

When Jesus had finished His work on earth, before He ascended to heaven, He commanded His followers to carry the gospel to every nation, to baptize the converts, and to teach them the Scriptures. "All authority has been given to Me in heaven and on earth," He told them, and He promised that He would always be with them, "even to the end of the age" (Matt. 28:18–20). Our authority to represent Jesus Christ comes from His authority, and that authority will never change or fail. Those who accept that authority and act upon it will receive all they need to serve Him, no matter what the circumstances may be.

Jesus knew the meaning of being under authority, for only those under authority should exercise authority. The Roman centurion understood our Lord's authority and therefore had great faith (Luke 7:1–10). Are we submitted to the Lord and obedient to His will? May the Father say of us as He said of Jesus, "I am well pleased." More about this in the following chapter.

(The Milestone Mirror: A Pause for Reflection)

Can you recall what life was like when you were twelve years old? Who were the important people in your life when you were on the threshold of your teen years? How did they treat you? Were you struggling for freedom? Did you secretly complain because nobody understood you?

When you had questions on your mind, to whom did you go for the answers? When you discussed things with others, did they respect your views? If they did not, how did you handle the matter?

Do you take time to answer the questions teens ask you today? Do you respect them?

If you were a believer in your early teens, did you seek counsel from the Lord through prayer and reading the Bible? Did you have anyone to guide you?

3

The Baptism of Jesus

Matthew 3:1–17; Mark 1:1–11; Luke 3:21–23

"How much of human life is lost in waiting!"

Ralph Waldo Emerson wrote that sentence in his essay "Prudence." Six years later he wrote in his journal, "The philosophy of waiting is sustained by all the oracles of the universe." I wonder what made him change his mind? After all, waiting is not wasting life but investing in personal character and the fulfillment of future hopes.

My family and close friends all know how impatient I can become when confronted by a delay, whether a traffic jam, a frozen airport passenger line, or even a supermarket checkout line. Whenever delays start upsetting me, I have to remind myself that I wrote a book called *God Isn't in a Hurry*. Then I confess my sins and ask the Lord for the grace to wait patiently. The Lord sometimes reminds me of Psalm 32:9, "Do not be like the horse or like the mule." The Lord wants us to be neither impulsive like the horse nor obstinate like the mule, but obedient like sheep following their Shepherd. Obedient waiting is not wasting time or smothering life. Obedient waiting means learning, maturing, and becoming what God wants us to be so we can do what He wants us to do.

After Jesus returned to Nazareth with Mary and Joseph, He waited eighteen years before beginning the three years of public ministry that climaxed at Calvary. But those were not wasted years. They were years of nurturing and maturing as He worked in the carpentry shop, attended synagogue services, assisted his mother Mary, communed with the Father, and increased in spiritual knowledge and insight. "He awakens Me morning by morning, He awakens My ear to hear as the learned" (Isa. 50:4). But when God's time came, Jesus said goodbye to Mary, siblings, and friends and headed for the Jordan River to be baptized by his cousin John, whose preaching was stirring up the nation and worrying the religious leaders.

As I meditated on this remarkable event, I saw three portraits of Jesus: the humble sojourner, the obedient servant, and the honored Son.

Jesus, the Humble Sojourner, Leaves Home

The day I was born, an ice storm paralyzed East Chicago, Indiana. I didn't cause it but it did cause problems for me. My father was unable to get my mother to the hospital and the doctor was delayed in getting to our home. By the goodness of God, one of my aunts was there and she and my father brought me into this world. I was born at home and I lived at that address for twenty-one years. Then my parents sold the house and we moved to a newer house in nearby Hammond, Indiana, where for three years I became a week-end visitor because I was attending seminary in Chicago. After seminary graduation, I was married and my wife and I settled into an apartment back in East Chicago, just a few blocks from the sanctuary of the Central Baptist Church, which I was pastoring. I won't bore you with facts about subsequent relocations because I want to get to my point, which is simply this: *everybody needs a place they can call home.*

In his poem "The Death of the Hired Man," Robert Frost says, "Home is the place where, when you have to go there, they have to take you in." But Jesus was *leaving* home, not starting a new home, and they had to let Him go. "Foxes have holes, and birds of the air have nests," He said, "but the Son of Man has nowhere to lay His head" (Luke 9:58). Jesus left His home in heaven to come to earth so that we who have trusted Him might one day have an eternal home in heaven. When He took that first step away from Nazareth, He was on His way to the cross. "He steadfastly set His face to go to Jerusalem" (Luke 9:51).

The Hebrew patriarchs were sojourners in the land. Abraham and Sarah left Ur of the Chaldees to go to the land God promised them, and Isaac and Jacob had their share of the pilgrim life. Jacob called his life "a pilgrimage" (Gen. 47:9) and died "leaning on the top of his staff" (Heb. 11:21), a traveler to the very end. During the years the people of Israel made their way to the Promised Land, they moved from place to place in the wilderness (Num. 33). "I am a stranger on the earth," said the Psalmist (119:19), and he too saw the life of faith as a pilgrimage (119:54). As David's life drew to a close, he worshiped the Lord and said, "For we are aliens and pilgrims before You, as were our fathers" (1 Chron. 29:15). The Old Testament believers "confessed that they were strangers and pilgrims on the earth" (Heb. 11:13).

The United States Department of Housing and Urban Development (HUD) did a one-night survey and discovered nearly 700,000 homeless people in the nation. Add to this the homeless in other nations and the numbers become alarming. My wife and I have traveled a great deal, but no matter where we have unpacked our luggage, *God was there with us,* for He is "our dwelling place in all generations" (Ps. 90:1). No matter what the new address might be, the most important thing was that the Landlord had not changed! Our gracious heavenly Father was with us wherever we lived and He never once failed us.

Christian believers today must confess that their citizenship is in heaven and so is their destination (Phil. 3:20–21). Peter addressed his first epistle to "the pilgrims of the Dispersion" (1:1) whose lives he called a "time of sojourning" (1:17). They were "sojourners and pilgrims" (2:11) who needed to live on earth as future residents of heaven. Paul points out that the Christian's body is but a temporary tent that will be taken down and replaced by a new body fit for the glorious heavenly home (2 Cor. 5:1–8).

Yes, Jesus was a humble sojourner during those three years of ministry. He knew what it was like to be hungry, weary, and thirsty (Mark 11:12; John 4:6–7), and what it felt like to suffer and die. Though He made Nazareth a headquarters city and then Capernaum, He was constantly on the move, without a bed to lie down in or a pillow for His head. Each occasional visit to the home of Mary, Martha, and Lazarus in Bethany must have been like an oasis in the desert to His tired body. And He did all of this for us!

We are supposed to live like sojourners, always on the move in our Christian life and not cluttered with extra baggage, what Mark Twain called "unnecessary necessities." We must be seeking to bring others with us on this journey to the heavenly city. No matter what may happen around us, we know that the Lord goes before us and prepares the way. We should "lay aside every weight, and the sin which so easily ensnares us" (Heb. 12:1), and follow the Lord on the paths He chooses for us. We should be humble sojourners.

Jesus, the Obedient Servant, Is Baptized

For four centuries, the people of Israel had not heard a true prophet, and then John the Baptist appeared at the Jordan River.

Great crowds went to hear him. He announced the arrival of the promised Messiah and the need for the people to repent, believe, and be baptized. The Jewish people were familiar with baptism because they required Gentile proselytes to the Jewish faith to be immersed in water; *but John was baptizing Jews!* When the Messiah appeared in the crowd to be baptized, John protested and said that Jesus ought to baptize him; but Jesus did not baptize anyone (John 4:2). Why, then, did Jesus, the sinless Lamb of God (John 1:29), insist that John baptize Him? Because this was His Father's will and demonstrated what would occur three years later on a hill called Calvary.

We must begin by recognizing that baptism in the New Testament was done by immersion, a fact that is acknowledged by scholars in a variety of denominations. The Greek word *baptizo* means "to dip, to immerse." Martin Luther wrote that "baptism is rather a symbol of death and resurrection. For this reason I would have those who are to be baptized completely immersed in the water."[1]

In his *Institutes of the Christian Religion*, John Calvin writes, "Yet the word 'baptize' means to immerse, and it is clear that the rite of immersion was observed in the ancient church."[2]

In *Wesley's Notes on the Bible,* John Wesley comments on Romans 6:4 ("We are buried with Him") by saying it is "alluding to the ancient manner of baptizing by immersion."[3]

The Catechism of the Catholic Church says, "Buried with Christ.... Baptism, the original and full sign of which is immersion,

---

[1]   *What Luther Says* (Saint Louis: Concordia Publishing House, 1959), 58.

[2]   John Calvin, *Institutes of the Christian Religion*, trans. Ford Lewis Battles; ed. John T. McNeill (Philadelphia: Westminster Press, 1960), 2: 1320.

[3]   *Wesley's Notes on the Bible* (Grand Rapids: Zondervan, 1987), 500.

efficaciously signifies the descent into the tomb by the Christian who dies to sin with Christ in order to live a new life."[4]

When he immersed Jesus in the Jordan River and brought Him up again, John was picturing our Lord's death, burial, and resurrection. It was by His death on the cross, His burial in the tomb, and His resurrection from the dead that the Son of God, with the Father and the Spirit, "fulfilled all righteousness" (Matt. 3:15). This is the gospel (1 Cor. 15:1–11). Jesus said that the only sign He would give to Israel was the sign of Jonah, which is death, burial, and resurrection (see Matt. 12:39–41; Luke 11:29–32). In his prayer, Jonah quoted from Psalm 42:7, "All Your billows and Your waves passed over me" (Jonah 2:3)—a picture of Jonah and Jesus in death, burial, and resurrection. Jesus Himself identified His sacrificial death as a baptism: "But I have a baptism to be baptized with, and how distressed I am until it is accomplished" (Luke 12:50).

The Father and the Son and the Holy Spirit worked together to accomplish our redemption. Jesus said to John, "for thus it is fitting for us [the Godhead] to fulfill all righteousness" (Matt. 3:15). In his hymn to the Trinity in Ephesians 1:3–14, Paul rejoices in the electing grace of the Father (vv. 3–6), the sacrificial death of the Son (vv. 7–12), and the sealing ministry of the Spirit (vv. 13–14). As far as the Father is concerned, I was saved when He chose me in Christ before the foundation of the world; as far as God the Son is concerned, I was saved when He died for me on the cross and arose again; and as far as God the Spirit is concerned, I was saved when He convicted me of my sins and gave me the faith to trust Jesus as Lord and Savior. The ministry of all three members of the Godhead is required to save the sinner. Paul's hymn

[4] *The Catechism of the Catholic Church* (New York: Doubleday, 1995), 179, para. 628.

is summarized in 1 Peter 1:2—"elect according to the foreknowledge [election] of God the Father, in sanctification of the Spirit, for obedience and sprinkling of the blood of Jesus Christ."

When Jesus accepted John's baptism, He was giving His approval of John's ministry. But the chief priests, scribes and elders rejected John's ministry, and when John was imprisoned, they did nothing to get him out. The religious leaders tried to trap Jesus one day and He silenced them by asking, "The baptism of John, where was it from? From heaven or from men?" (Matt. 21:23–27). Had the religious leaders received the ministry of John, they would have been prepared to receive their Messiah and be saved, but they wasted their opportunity.

In His baptism, Jesus identified Himself with sinners, just as He did in His daily ministry (Matt. 9:9–13) and especially in His death on the cross (Matt. 27:38). In life and in death our Lord was "numbered with the transgressors" (Isa. 53:12). How tragic it is that some believers have changed the word "separation" to "isolation" and alienated themselves from the lost people who desperately need their loving witness (Matt. 9:9–13).

Jesus, the Encouraged Son, Is Honored

All of us need encouragement in our lives and ministries, and the Son of Man was about to go into the wilderness to be tempted by the devil. After that He would be opposed by the religious leaders who should have fallen at His feet and worshiped Him. It doesn't surprise us that Jesus prayed during His baptism (Luke 3:21–22), for He was truly a Man of prayer. Luke records eight occasions of our Lord's praying (3:21; 5:16; 6:12; 9:18, 29; 11:1; 23:34, 46). He awakened early each morning and spent time praying and communing with the Father (Mark 1:34–35; Luke 5:15–16). He prayed all night before He chose the twelve apostles (Luke 6:12–13), a good example for us to follow when we must make decisions, whether great or small. He prayed at the transfiguration (Luke 9:28–29), in the garden of Gethsemane (Luke 22:39–46), while being crucified (Luke 23:34), and while hanging on the cross (Matt. 27:46; Luke 23:46). John 17 records perhaps the greatest prayer in the Scriptures.

The people in the crowd were ignorant of the fact that the Son of God was in their midst, and they had no word of encouragement for Him; but the Father spoke from heaven, "This is My beloved Son, in whom I am well pleased" (Matt. 3:17).

In my own Christian walk, there have been times when God's Word from Scripture has been exactly the tonic I needed. The Gospel writers mention three occasions when the Father addressed the Son from heaven and encouraged Him: here at His baptism, on the mount of transfiguration (Matt. 17:5), and after our Lord's triumphal entry into Jerusalem (John 12:27–36).

Note that the Father spoke audibly to Jesus at the beginning of His ministry, in the middle of His ministry and as His ministry drew to a close. I have never heard God speak audibly from heaven, but He has spoken to me from Scripture, through the lips of other believers, through the verse of a song, and from difficult and challenging circumstances. "He that has ears to hear, let him hear" (Matt. 13:9).

Jesus was encouraged not only by the fact that His Father spoke to Him but also by what the Father said to Him. He called Jesus His "beloved Son" and He assured Jesus that He was well pleased with Him. During those thirty years in Nazareth, Jesus had always pleased the Father. This affirmation of love and joy would help carry Jesus through those forty days in the wilderness when He was being tempted by Satan. God's love for us and His approval of our walk and our work are great sources of strength and endurance. Often when we are in pain or sorrow, Satan says to us, "If God loves you so much, why are you suffering? This is a strange way for Him to show His love!" But then the Father speaks from the Word of God and affirms His love for us and His joy over our obedience. Even more, we can feel the love of God in our hearts, especially when a fellow Christian shares God's love with us.

The Father was well pleased with the Son, and it should be our concern daily to please the Father in everything. "The Father has not left Me alone," said Jesus, "for I always do those things that please Him" (John 8:29). Doing what pleases God may not always please others, but Peter reminds us that our duty is "to obey God rather than men" (Acts 5:29).

Jesus was honored by the voice of the Father and by His loving commendation, but He was also honored by the presence of the Holy Spirit who descended like a dove and rested upon Him. The Father and the Son and the Holy Spirit were united in "fulfilling all righteousness" (Matt. 3:13–15), and the dove's alighting on Jesus identified Him as the holy Son of God (John 1:33–34). One of the ministries of the Holy Spirit in this world today is to point to Jesus and glorify Him (John 16:14). From our Lord's conception to His resurrection, the Holy Spirit empowered Jesus and enabled Him to know and do the will of God. Remember, Jesus lived on this earth just as every Christian must live—trusting the word of God, praying, obeying the will of God, and depending on the power of the Holy Spirit.

Years ago, I heard Dr. A. W. Tozer say, "If God were to take the Holy Spirit out of this world, most of what the church is doing would go right on *and nobody would know the difference.*" For our Lord's first recorded sermon in His hometown of Nazareth, He chose Isaiah 61:1–2 as His text, as reported in Luke 4:18–20:

The Spirit of the Lord is upon Me, because He has anointed Me to preach the gospel to the poor, He has sent Me to heal the brokenhearted, to preach deliverance to the captives and recovery of sight to the blind, to set at liberty those who are oppressed, to preach the acceptable year of the Lord.

Jesus ministered to people who needed His help so desperately—the poor, the brokenhearted, the captives, the blind, and the oppressed. These afflictions still burden people in our modern world and only Jesus can help them handle those burdens. Before Jesus returned to heaven, His disciples asked Him if He was going to restore the kingdom to Israel, and He told them not to look back but to look ahead to all the new things He would do in and through them (Acts 1:4–8). That the Spirit took the form of a dove reminds us of the Spirit's purity, loyalty, gentleness, and peacefulness. As God's people, we are to be "wise as serpents and harmless as doves" (Matt. 10:16), and we must manifest the fruit of the Spirit in all that we do (Gal. 5:22–23).

If our Lord Jesus Christ, with all His perfections, had to depend on the Holy Spirit for power to serve, how much more do we limited and sinful humans need the Spirit! Many congregations recite the Apostles' Creed when they celebrate the Lord's Supper, and say together, "I believe in the Holy Spirit," but is there any evidence that the Spirit is at work in their lives and in the church's ministry? Or are we like the believers in Sardis who had a name that they were alive but were actually spiritually dead (Rev. 3:1–6)? Yes, it's possible to imitate some of the works of the Holy Spirit and make people think we are "on fire for God," but apart from the "Spirit of life in Christ Jesus" (Rom. 8:2) we cannot live a life like that of Christ Jesus.

(*The Milestone Mirror: A Pause for Reflection*)

When it came time to step out on your own, whether to employment or further education, how did you feel? Was it painful or a relief? What assurance did you have that you were in God's will?

When and how did you publicly declare your faith in Jesus Christ? How do you declare your faith today?

Is there a strong motivation in your heart to please your heavenly Father?

Have you learned to discover God's will through prayer and meditating on God's Word?

The Temptation of Jesus

Matthew 4:1–11; Mark 1:12–13; Luke 4:1–13

During His ministry on earth, our Lord lived by faith, just as God's children must do today. "For we walk by faith, not by sight" (2 Cor. 5:7), and faith is living without scheming. Jesus trusted the Scriptures, the power of the Holy Spirit, and the character of His heavenly Father to whom He prayed. He knew the Scriptures were true, that the Father was faithful, and that the Spirit would not desert Him; therefore, He was able to face His daily tasks and challenges with confidence.

But living by faith also involves experiencing trials, for a faith that can't be tested can't be trusted. The Christian life is like the Promised Land God gave to Israel, "a land of hills and valleys" (Deut. 11:11). Our Lord's baptism was an awesome experience as He heard the Father speak from heaven and saw the Spirit come down like a dove; but this mountain-top experience was followed by forty days of fasting in the wilderness climaxed by Satan attacking Him with three crafty temptations. Whenever we are blessed in a special way, we can be sure the enemy is just around the corner waiting to attack. While we are rejoicing in God's blessings, we must be careful not to start trusting our feelings and start neglecting our responsibilities, especially our responsibility to obey the Lord and not be deceived and detoured by Satan's schemes.

God tests us so He can enrich us and build us up, but Satan tempts us so he can rob us and tear us down. *The decisions we make determine whether we profit from God's tests or turn the test into a temptation.* A test is a God-given opportunity to experience God's love and grace and win a victory, but Satan always has an alternative plan that seems very inviting. A temptation is an opportunity from Satan to experience a legitimate pleasure but get it in an illegitimate way. It's a good thing to pass a final exam, but it's a sin to "borrow" your answers from that intelligent student sitting next to you. It's good and proper to save money, but not by cheating on your income tax return. Yielding to temptation seems harmless and clever at the time, but the ultimate damage to our character and our walk with God demonstrates how foolish and costly it is.

When praying the Lord's Prayer, we ask, "And do not lead us into temptation" (Matt. 6:13); but Matthew 4:1 says, "Then Jesus was led up by the Spirit into the wilderness to be tempted by the devil." The Father was not *tempting* the Son to sin, for God cannot be tempted; the Father was *testing* Him, knowing that Jesus would be victorious (James 1:12–15).

Let's consider Satan's strategy in these three temptations and how Jesus defeated him.

"Turn These Stones into Bread" (Matthew 4:1–4)

Forty days before Satan appeared to Him, Jesus heard His Father affirm both His love and His approval, and now the devil was questioning what God had said. "If the Father loves You so much, why are You hungry? If He is well-pleased with You, why must You suffer?" Satan is questioning God's word and God's character just as he did with Eve when he tempted her (Gen. 3:1–6). "Is it true that God won't allow you to eat of *every* tree in the garden?

But if God really loved you, He wouldn't deprive you like that."
Once Eve began to doubt God's word and love, it was easy for
Satan to deny God's word and then to substitute his own life
(Gen. 3:4–5).

But the devil's approach to Jesus was even more subtle, for he
knows the power Jesus possesses as the Son of God. *Satan suggested that Jesus use His own power to meet His own needs and not to
glorify the Father by serving others!* "Isn't preservation the first law
of life? If Your Father isn't caring for You, You have the right to
care for Yourself."

This kind of reasoning motivates dictators and other "control freaks," the people who think they have the right to domi-
nate others and have their own way or else. But Jesus said, "I am
among you as the One who serves" (Luke 22:27). Jesus took the
form of a servant and humbled Himself that He might serve others, even to the point of sacrificing Himself for us on the cross
(Phil. 2:5–11). First the suffering and then the glory has always
been God's order. Paul wrote, "For I consider that the sufferings
of this present time are not worthy to be compared with the glory
which shall be revealed in us" (Rom. 8:18).

With only a word, Jesus could easily have turned stones into
bread, but that was not the Father's will. "Man shall not live by
bread alone, but by every word that proceeds from the mouth of
God" (Matt. 4:4). Jesus merely quoted from Deuteronomy 8:3.
To Jesus, hunger was not punishment. He knew He was doing the
Father's will and *the Father's will is nourishment!*

This parallels John 4:34, "My food is to do the will of Him
who sent Me, and to finish His work." Satan wants us to believe
that every pain, disappointment, or traffic jam is evidence of
God's displeasure with us, but the clear statements in the Scriptures and the witness of the Spirit in our hearts assure us of God's
love and care. David advised us, "Cast your burden on the Lord,
and He shall sustain you" (Ps. 55:22), and Peter wrote, "Casting all

your care upon Him, for He cares for you" (1 Peter 5:7). Living by faith means obeying God and resting on God's word no matter what the circumstances might be around us, the consequences before us, or the feelings within us.

Let's meditate on the fact that the Scriptures are nourishment to the inner person just as food is nourishment to the body. Moses compared the Scriptures to bread (Deut. 8:3), but the psalmists also compared God's word to honey (Pss. 19:9–10; 119:103); and Peter wrote, "As newborn babes, desire the pure milk of the word that you may grow thereby" (1 Peter 2:2). Healthy babies have an insatiable appetite for their mother's milk, but Paul counsels us to mature spiritually and desire the "solid food" of the word (1 Cor. 3:1–3; see Heb. 5:11–14). The milk of the word records what Jesus said and did when He was ministering on earth, but the solid food of Scripture is what Jesus says and does now as our high priest. Christians who digest a daily diet of God's word will grow in grace and knowledge (2 Peter 3:18) and be able to detect and defeat Satan's subtle attacks.

David wrote, "I have been young, and now am old; yet I have not seen the righteous forsaken, nor his descendants begging bread" (Ps. 37:25). Our victories today will bring blessings to our descendants tomorrow, but our defeats may bring them sorrow. Abraham arrived in Canaan only to find a famine, and instead of remaining there and trusting the Lord, he fled to Egypt and got into trouble. What Abraham did eventually influenced his nephew Lot who made some unwise decisions and ended in shameful ruin (Gen. 12:16–13:13; 19). The next time we are tempted by the devil, let's ignore present pleasures and consider future consequences that may come to us and our descendants.

"Throw Yourself Down from the Temple" (Matthew 4:5–7)

Satan began his attack by questioning the Father's love for His Son; and now he questions the very truth of God itself. In the first attack, Jesus defeated the evil one by quoting Scripture, so Satan retaliates by also quoting Scripture. (Yes, the devil knows the Bible!) Satan's text is Psalm 91:11 and 12, but he avoids verse 13, which promises the believer victory over lions and cobras. After all, Satan is the serpent and the lion, the deceiver and the devourer (2 Cor. 11:3; 1 Peter 5:8). "You say that Your life is guided and nourished by the word of God. Prove it! Claim this promise and see if the angels will protect You! When the people see you accomplish this great feat, they will follow You."

Jesus had a human body that could die, and it would die on the cross. If He leaped off the pinnacle of the temple, He would be tempting the Father to protect Him; so He defeated the devil by quoting Deuteronomy 6:16: "You shall not tempt the Lord your God." To tempt the Lord is to deliberately put yourself in a disobedient and dangerous situation and expect God to rescue you. It means daring God to act at your command. You might even find a verse in the Bible that supports your outrageous decision, but that is not reason enough for doing it. Jesus said to Satan, "It is written again" (Matt. 4:7). Note that word "again." It commands us to balance Scripture with Scripture, because if you take verses out of context, you can prove almost anything.

I think it was G. Campbell Morgan who told about the man who sought the will of God by randomly opening his Bible and, with his eyes closed, pointing to a verse. The first time he did it, the verse said, "Then he [Judas] . . . went and hanged himself" (Matt. 27:5). He closed the Bible and tried again; this time he pointed to Luke 10:37, "Go and do likewise." His third attempt gave him John 13:27, "What you do, do quickly."

One of the first axioms of hermeneutics (the principles of Bible study) is, "A text without a context is a pretext." I read about one notable preacher who wanted to know if he should ask his girlfriend to marry him, and he opened his Bible and blindly pointed to Ezekiel 37:17 where the two sticks became one in the hands of the prophet. Two became one, so the answer must be "Marry her!"

There is no substitute for reading the whole Bible over and over, meditating on it, and tracing the cross references. "All Scripture is given by inspiration of God" (2 Tim. 3:16), and we dare not overlook any part of it, for one part helps us better understand another part.

Satan could quote Psalm 91:11–12, but Jesus answered him with Deuteronomy 6:16. The full verse reads, "You shall not tempt the LORD your God as you tempted Him in Massah." Jesus did not quote that last phrase, but I recommend you read Exodus 17:1–7 to get the full force of the verse. As Israel marched through the wilderness, they came to Rephidim and were thirsty, but there was no water there. The people complained bitterly against Moses and by doing so criticized God. They were actually tempting God to discipline them, but in His grace He provided the water. Moses changed the name of the place from Rephidim ("plains") to Massah, which means "tempted." When circumstances are difficult, how prone we are to complain to the Lord, and this is the equivalent of tempting the Lord. We should be praising the Lord and asking Him for grace to glorify Him. Immature people complain and ask, "How can I get out of this?" Mature people pray and ask, "*What* can I get out of this? "For you have need of endurance, so that after you have done the will of God, you may receive the promise" (Heb. 10:36; cf. 6:12).

When we pray "lead us not into temptation," we are really saying, "Lord, don't let me tempt You or tempt myself or tempt others." When Lot moved into the wicked city of Sodom, he was tempting himself and his family, and so was Samson when he entangled himself with Delilah. When Jesus was arrested in the garden, He told His disciples to go their own way (John 18:8); but

Peter disobeyed and followed. He walked right into temptation and denied the Lord three times.

As for tempting others to sin, Matthew 18:1–9 contains some stern warnings. Psalm 1:1 pictures a man getting into sin because he deliberately kept the wrong company. The Lord promises to give us victory over temptation if we really want to obey Him (1 Cor. 10:13). He knows how much we can bear and will provide a way of escape if we trust Him.

"Worship Me!" (Matthew 4:8–11)

So far in this study we have seen Satan questioning God and tempting God. Now he will seek to replace God, because the devil's ambition has always been to "be like the Most High" (Isa. 14:12–14). It comes as a shock to some believers to discover that Satan is being worshiped not only in so-called pagan temples, but also in buildings dedicated to the Lord by people who call themselves "Christians." I have attended services where Jesus was not exalted in either the music or the preaching and there was no evidence of the fear of the Lord. Remember, Satan is a counterfeiter and knows how to imitate much of what God commands His people to do.

Jesus called Satan "the ruler of this world" (John 12:31; 14:30), indicating that the devil has limited authority in our world today. Satan has counterfeit ministers (2 Cor. 11:1–4, 13–15) who preach a counterfeit gospel (Gal. 1:6–9) in counterfeit churches (Rev. 2:9; 3:9). He offers a counterfeit righteousness that is based on good works and not on the finished work of Christ on the cross (Rom. 10:1–13). Our enemy doesn't like it when Christians truly worship the Lord together, read and study the Bible, and pray for one another—for those in authority and for people who need to be saved. He also doesn't want us to help the helpless or care for the needy.

But the cross is another factor involved in this temptation. Jesus will one day reign as King of kings and Lord of lords because He died on the cross and paid the price for our sins. He arose from the dead and ascended to His throne in heaven. The Lord is allowing Satan a limited amount of freedom, but one day that will end and Satan and his hosts will be imprisoned in the lake of fire forever (Rev. 19–20). Because Jesus has defeated Satan (Col. 2:11–15), God's people can claim daily victory in their living and reigning Redeemer.

This temptation was one of Satan's devices to try to keep Jesus from dying on the cross and defeating the whole Satanic system. If He worshiped the evil one, Jesus would temporarily receive the glory of the world's kingdoms and not have to suffer and die, but Satan's glory does not last. His temptations appear to be easy shortcuts toward achieving a good purpose, but there are no shortcuts in the Christian life. The biblical way toward glory begins with suffering. When Jesus announced to the twelve apostles that He would suffer in Jerusalem and be crucified, Peter's response was, "Far be it from You, Lord; this shall not happen to You!" Our Lord's response was, "Get behind Me, Satan!" (Matt. 16:21–23). Yes, Satan sometimes uses believers to speak his lies, and we must exercise discernment. But Peter learned his lesson, for in his first epistle, he explains the relationship between suffering and glory in the Christian life. Churches today need to study 1 Peter, because persecution is coming and many Christians are not prepared to meet it.

There was another time when Satan tempted Jesus to abandon the cross. After feeding the five thousand, Jesus detected that the crowd wanted to make Him king, but He dismissed them and went up on the mountain to pray (John 6:15). Jesus knew that the cross must precede the crown. None of us enjoys suffering, but if we want to glorify our Lord, we must suffer and trust the

Holy Spirit to enable us to honor Jesus (1 Peter 4:12–19). "For I consider that the sufferings of this present time are not worthy to be compared with the glory which shall be revealed in us" (Rom. 8:18).

Jesus silenced the devil by quoting Deuteronomy 6:13, but it is interesting to note that Jesus mentioned "service" as well as "worship." Satan had said nothing about service but Jesus did, for He knew that *whatever we serve sacrificially is what we worship.* If we truly love God, we will make sacrifices in order to serve Him. After Peter tried to remove the crucifixion from our Lord's agenda, he heard Jesus say, "If any man desires to come after Me, let him deny himself, and take up his cross, and follow Me" (Matt. 16:24). Suddenly Peter discovered that he also had a cross to bear! If we bypass the cross, we forfeit much blessing, for then we know nothing of "the fellowship of His sufferings" (Phil. 3:10).

Those who understand suffering and glory will also understand how to "reign in life through the One, Jesus Christ" (Rom. 5:17). When God created Adam and Eve, He gave them dominion over the fish, the birds, and the animals (Gen. 1:26–31; Ps. 8); but they lost their dominion when they disobeyed God. When Jesus came to earth, He demonstrated that He indeed was the king, for He had control over the fish (Luke 5:1–11; Matt. 17:24–27; John 21:1–14), the birds (Mark 14:27–31, 66–72), and the beasts (Mark 1:12–13; 11:1–3). When our Lord establishes His kingdom on earth, all nature will obey Him and there will be no conflicts (Isa. 11:1–9).

* * *

There will come a day when Satan will say to a man, "If you will worship me, I will give you all the world's kingdoms and glory." The man will accept the offer *and the Antichrist will be on the scene!* Bible students don't agree on all the details of Revelation 12–19, but the big picture is clear. Posing as a peacemaker, this counterfeit Christ will be admired and accepted by the world and ultimately worshiped by the world. He will persecute and kill many of God's people and control the world economy, politics, and religion. God will send judgments upon his kingdom, but in spite of pain and social upheaval, Antichrist's people will not repent of their sins (Rev. 16:8–11). Antichrist and his forces will unite to attack God's people, but then Jesus will come from heaven with His hosts and put Antichrist and his associates into the lake of fire. Jesus will establish His kingdom on earth and His servants will serve Him.

Victory Now!

But our concern should be to serve Christ *now* and have victory over Satan and his demonic army *now* (Eph. 6:10–20). Each day we must put on the whole armor of God, we must take up the sword of the word of God and the shield of faith, and we must battle whenever Satan attacks us and our fellow believers. We must devote time to prayer, individually and in groups, and we must ask God to glorify Himself in the overthrow of the devil. When I read the Acts of the Apostles, I'm impressed with the prayer ministry of the early church and with the answers God granted them. It grieves me that prayer doesn't seem to be emphasized in some churches today.

Did you notice what happened after Jesus had won the battle against Satan? "Then the devil left Him, and behold, angels came and ministered to Him" (Matt. 4:11). Luke 4:13 tells us that Satan "departed from Him until a more opportune time," for he is alert to find footholds in our lives. (And we should be alert to get rid of them!) I doubt that Satan has ever attacked me personally, because I'm not on his "most wanted" list. Mention my name and the demon would say, "Jesus I know, and Paul I know; but who is Wiersbe?" (see Acts 19:15). *But I have available to me all that I need to discern the devil's tactics and defeat him!* And the angels will minister to me when I need them (Heb. 1:14). The angels protected Daniel (Dan. 6:22), liberated Peter (Acts 12), guided Philip (Acts 8:26–40), and helped the apostle John write the last book in the Bible (Rev. 1:1–3). Angels are our servants, and though we must not worship them or pray to them, we may trust them to help us as our Father commands them.

What gave Jesus victory also gives us victory. For one thing, He was in the Father's will and the Father was pleased with Him. Christians who are out of God's will are perfect targets for the devil and they often end up tempting themselves. Our Lord was filled with the Spirit of God and the word of God and was able to use the Scriptures He needed to silence Satan. "Your word I have hidden in my heart, that I might not sin against You" (Ps. 119:11). He prayed and trusted the Father to answer, and He did! The spiritual armor is the equipment we need for battle, but prayer and the Holy Spirit provide the enablement we need to use our equipment effectively: "Praying always with all prayer and supplication in the Spirit" (Eph. 6:16).

"No temptation has overtaken you except such as is common to man; but God is faithful, who will not allow you to be tempted beyond what you are able, but with the temptation will also make the way of escape, that you may be able to bear it" (1 Cor. 10:13).

Jesus has already won the victory, so let's claim it by faith.

(The Milestone Mirror: A Pause for Reflection)

Have you learned that sometimes a glorious experience with the Lord might be followed by a battle with temptation? Why do you think the Father permits this sequence?

It is not a sin to be tempted, for the sinless Son of God was tempted; but it is dangerous to "play" with temptation and give it consideration. How do you distinguish between the devil's temptations and the Father's tests?

Our Lord's example makes it clear that the word of God is the best weapon for overcoming the evil one (Eph. 6:10–18; Heb. 4:12). Have you memorized Scripture so that you have your ammunition ready? (See Ps. 119:11.)

When Satan tempts you, do you claim 1 Corinthians 10:13 and ask your Father to help you use "the way out"? Do you have a daily quiet time with the Lord, meditating on the Scriptures, praying, and seeking God's directions for the day?

Is there one particular temptation that repeatedly confronts you? Have you discussed this with another Christian?

We pray in the Lord's Prayer (Matt. 6:9–15), "And do not lead us into temptation." The Lord does not tempt us (James 1:12–18), but if we fail to say a decisive "No!" to the devil's offers, we may start tempting ourselves, tempting others, or even tempting the Lord! To even consider yielding to temptation is to reject the help the Lord can give us.

5

The Transfiguration of Jesus

Matthew 17:1–13; Mark 9:2–13; Luke 9:28–36

The Greek word translated "transfigured" gives us the English word "metamorphosis," which means a change on the outside that comes from the inside. When Jesus began to shine, it was not because the angels in heaven had turned a powerful spotlight on Him. It was because His divine nature was radiating through His body and His raiment. The larva going into the cocoon and coming out a butterfly has experienced metamorphosis. Jesus revealed His divine nature in its glory, an awesome event beheld only by the Father in heaven and five persons on earth: Peter, James, John, Moses, and Elijah. It is our privilege to learn some basic spiritual lessons from what they saw on the high mountain.

Jesus and the Crowds

Frequently in the Gospel records we read that large crowds of people followed Jesus, no matter where He went. Some came to experience His miraculous healing power, others to see those miracles performed, and still others to hear Him teach spiritual truth. Jesus couldn't ignore the crowds because He came to earth to minister to people and bring them the good news of the kingdom. I used to tell pastors in conferences, "We want crowds, not so we can count people but because people count and we want to serve them."

Some celebrities in their press interviews have admitted that enthusiastic crowds wear them down and, if they don't escape from their public now and then, they can't live at their best. Each morning Jesus would rise early and go to a solitary place to pray (Mark 1:35). Our Lord occasionally took His disciples with Him, slipped away from the crowds, and found rest and refreshment in solitude. We call this a "retreat," but even then the crowds found Him (Mark 6:30–44). The remarkable "transfiguration retreat" reported by Matthew, Mark, and Luke took Jesus away from the pressing throngs and gave Him opportunity to glorify the Father and prepare Himself and three of His disciples for His approaching suffering and death.

We live these days in a fast-moving, crowd-controlled world, and if we aren't careful, we may be captured by the crowd and gradually lose our identity. Philosopher Blaise Pascal wrote, "All the unhappiness of men arises from one single fact that they cannot stay quietly in their own chamber" (*Pensees* #139). If we can't get along with ourselves, we can never conquer the crowd. In his autobiography *Out of My Later Years*, Albert Einstein wrote, "I lived in solitude in the country and noticed how the monotony of a quiet life stimulates the creative mind."[1] The American naturalist and poet Henry David Thoreau wrote in the "Economy" chapter of *Walden*, "I would rather sit on a pumpkin and have it all to myself than be crowded on a velvet cushion." We can spend so much time with others that we fail to spend adequate time with ourselves and the Lord.

---

[1]   Albert Einstein, *Out of My Later Years* (New York: Citadel Press, 2000), 24.

Solitude is not the same as isolation or loneliness. Many people can be in the middle of a noisy crowd and yet feel very lonely. It's the person with a balanced life, walking with God, who can handle both the crowd and the cloister. In fact, those who find enrichment in solitude have something to share with the crowd. Jesus was not alone on the mountain, for Peter, James, and John were with Him at His request; then Moses and Elijah appeared, and the Father spoke from heaven. The divine promise to God's people is, "I will never leave you nor forsake you" (Joshua 1:5; Heb. 13:5). As believers, we can overcome the destructive influences of the worldly crowd because we spend time alone with the Lord. The blessed life is a balanced life, and the Lord is the one who keeps everything in control. Those who in the solitary place have found peace in Christ will have no problem finding that same peace in the crowd.

In his essay "The Decline of Heroes," historian Arthur M. Schlesinger Jr. wrote: "If we are to survive, we must have ideas, vision, courage. These things are rarely produced by committees. Everything that matters in our intellectual and moral life begins with an individual confronting his own mind and conscience in a room by himself."[2] It takes both society and solitude, the mountaintop and the valley, to make us mature, creative people, and with the Lord's help, we can handle both. Blessed are the balanced.

Jesus and the Glory

In the ancient Near East, the Gentile nations had temples, priests, and rituals, but only the nation of Israel had God's glory dwelling in their sanctuary (Rom. 9:4). When Moses dedicated the tabernacle, God's glory moved in (Exod. 40:34–38), and when Solomon

---

[2]   *Adventures of the Mind*, ed. Richard Thruelson and John Kobler (New York: Alfred A. Knopf, 1960), 103.

dedicated the temple, the glory filled the house (2 Chron. 7:1–3). The idols of the nations were without life or glory and could do nothing, but the living God of Israel is glorious in everything He is, says, and does!

The tragedy is that, over the centuries, the people of Israel repeatedly sinned against the Lord and even put idols in His temple; and eventually the glory of God departed from the sanctuary. The prophet Ezekiel records how the glory moved from the mercy seat in the holy of holies to above the threshold of the temple, then to the eastern gate, and from there it left the temple completely and went over the Mount of Olives (Ezek. 10:1–19; 11:22–23). The priests could have written "Ichabod" over the temple, "the glory has departed" (1 Sam. 4:19–22). Ezekiel also revealed that the glory would return and dwell in the temple in the future kingdom (43:1–5).

When Jesus was born in Bethlehem, God's glory returned to the people of Israel in the person of the Son of God (Luke 2:8–9). "And the Word became flesh and dwelt among us, and we beheld His glory" (John 1:14). Jesus glorified God in His life, teachings, and miracles, and especially in His death and resurrection. But the transfiguration of Jesus on the mount was very special and has significance for us today. When Jesus was born, He was wrapped in strips of cloth called "swaddling clothes," and when He was buried, Joseph of Arimathea and Nicodemus wrapped Him in strips of linen. But on the mount, Jesus radiated His glory in a way His disciples had never seen before. This glory revealed that Jesus is indeed the Son of God.

We must note that Jesus was praying as this remarkable event transpired (Luke 9:29). Our daily times of fellowship with the Lord ought to send us forth radiating the presence of God as we serve others and seek to honor Christ. Whether we like it or not, our faces often reflect our character and attitudes; and how wonderful it would be if we all had shining faces! While Stephen was being stoned to death, he prayed for his executioners, and "his face was as the face of an angel" (Acts 6:15). We can use soap, water, and cosmetics to deal with facial blemishes, but the best "beauty treatment" is a heart full of love, a will yielded to the Spirit, and a mind full of God's truth. "Prayer changes things" is a familiar saying, but prayer also changes us! If we want the glory of God to transfigure us, we had better spend quality time in prayer.

Jesus was on His way to Calvary, and His transfiguration reminded Him that the suffering He would endure would ultimately lead to glory. It was a revelation of the glory of His coming kingdom (Matt. 16:27–28) when the cross would be replaced by the crown (Heb. 2:9). After His resurrection, Jesus asked the two Emmaus disciples, "Ought not the Christ to have suffered these things and to enter into His glory?" (Luke 24:26). Too many believers think that suffering in the will of God is a strange thing, for, if we are obeying God, He ought to shelter us. When Peter first heard that the Master would die on a cross, his response was, "Far be it from you, Lord"; and Jesus rebuked him (Matt. 16:21–23). Suffering is one of God's tools for preparing us for glory, not only today but when Jesus returns (1 Peter 4:13).

Those who have trusted Jesus Christ already have His glory in the person of the Holy Spirit within them (John 17:22; 1 Peter 4:14), and that glory is revealed in the way we live and the works we do (Matt. 5:16). It will be revealed when we reach our heavenly home, see Jesus, and rejoice in His presence. Meanwhile, we walk by faith, knowing that the Lord always keeps His promises. Charles Spurgeon said that the promises of God shine the brightest in the furnace of affliction, and he was right. Suffering and glory go together as do God's grace and our suffering. "The Lord will give grace and glory" (Ps. 84:11).

Jesus and the Heavenly Visitors

Not only was the Master radiant with divine glory, but so were two men who suddenly appeared and conversed with Jesus about "His decease which He was about to accomplish in Jerusalem" (Luke 9:31). The three disciples knew who these men were because this was another manifestation of heavenly glory, and in heaven we shall know one another even as we are known. Moses represented the law and Elijah the prophets, for in Jesus we see the fulfillment of the law and the prophets (Matt. 5:17). "For the law was given through Moses, but grace and truth came through Jesus Christ" (John 1:17). Because he disobeyed the Lord, Moses was not permitted to enter the Promised Land before he died (Num. 20:1–13; Deut. 34:1–4), but there he was on a mountaintop in Israel with the Son of God!

The word translated "decease" is the Greek word *exodus*, a suitable word for the topic of conversation Jesus was having with Moses and Elijah (Luke 9:30–31). Moses supervised the exodus of Israel out of Egyptian slavery, Elijah led the unfaithful nation out of pagan idolatry and back to the Lord (1 Kings 18). Jesus accomplished the most important exodus of all, for He delivers lost sinners from the power of darkness and takes them into His glorious kingdom (Col. 1:13). In the days of Moses in Egypt, it was the blood of the lamb that protected the Jews from death and enabled them to go free, and it is the blood of God's Lamb today that sets us free (John 1:29; Eph. 1:7). Jesus became a prisoner that we might be set free, and one day He will take His bride, the church, far above the mountaintops and into the glory of heaven! Elijah did not close his ministry by dying but was carried alive into heaven, just as God's people who are alive at Christ's return will be caught up to glory after the dead are raised (2 Kings

2:9–12; 1 Thess. 4:13–18). What a marvelous day that will be, and it will mean glory forever!

It must have been encouraging to the three disciples to see Moses and Elijah sharing the glory as they spoke with Jesus, for neither the two prophets nor the three disciples had perfect records of service. Jesus didn't bring up any of their mistakes or failures, for God says of His people, "Their sins and their lawless deeds I will remember no more" (Heb. 8:12; 10:17). Moses and Elijah had ministries to perform even after they had gone to heaven, and so shall all of God's children when we see the Lord (Rev. 22:3).

I don't expect Moses or Elijah to visit me, *but I can visit them!* As I read and meditate on the Scriptures, I can be helped and challenged by the servants of God who are now in heaven. Have we ever been disobedient to the Lord? So were they, but God forgave them, restored them, and continued to use them for His glory. Both Moses and Elijah each became so discouraged in their work that they wanted to die! (See Num. 11:1–15 and 1 Kings 19:1–18.) The Lord didn't reject them; He simply quieted their hearts and assured them their work was not in vain. Many times the Lord has spoken to me as I have read about Abraham, David, Ruth, Jeremiah, and Jesus and the apostles. I don't live in the past, *but the past lives in me as the Holy Spirit reminds me of what I have been taught!* (see John 14:26).

Jesus and the Three Disciples

This is the second time Jesus took Peter, James, and John with Him on a special ministry. The first occurred when He raised the daughter of Jairus from the dead (Luke 8:51–56), and the third would be when Jesus went into the garden to pray (Matt. 26:37). It has been pointed out that each of these occasions was connected with death. In the home of Jairus, Jesus showed Himself as the conqueror of death; on the mount of transfiguration He was seen glorified in death; and in the garden, He showed Himself surrendered to the Father's will in His death.

During His years of ministry, Jesus not only taught the multitudes, but He also taught His disciples and prepared them for the future ministries they would have after He had returned to heaven. He said to the Father, "I have glorified You on the earth. I have finished the work which You have given Me to do" (John 17:4). This is not referring to His death on the cross for He had not yet been arrested and tried. It is referring to His work of training the disciples. In John 17:6–19, He prayed for His disciples, that they would glorify Him by being effective in their ministries. Jesus had given them the word of God and taught them about the Father and the Spirit whom they would receive forty days after His resurrection.

But why did He select Peter, James, and John to witness this event? Because each of them would have a distinctive ministry and be examples for us to follow. He prepared Peter to be a leader (Luke 22:32), James to be a martyr (Acts 12:1–2), and John to be a teacher (John 20:30–31), and each of their ministries would glorify the Lord. James was the first martyr of the Christian church and Peter was the leader of the church in the opening years of its witness (Acts 1–12).

In his letters, Peter prepared the churches in the Roman Empire for the persecution they would face. During his long life, the apostle John was inspired by the Spirit to write his Gospel, three epistles, and the book of the Revelation of Jesus Christ, which he wrote when a Roman prisoner on the island of Patmos. John's words in Revelation 1:5–6 summarize his writings: "To Him who loved us" (the Gospel of John), "and washed us [freed us] from our sins in His own blood" (the epistles of John), "and has made us kings and priests" (the book of Revelation). John's teaching ministry focuses on the past, present, and future.

The three disciples were "heavy with sleep" (Luke 9:32), a fault they repeated in the garden (Luke 22:45); but when Peter was fully awake, he realized that Moses and Elijah were leaving. His suggestion that he build booths for Jesus and His guests was evidence that his mind was still confused because he didn't really know what he was saying. But while Peter was still speaking, the Father interrupted him by placing a cloud over them and speaking to them. Peter was interrupted here by the Father and later by the Son (Matt. 17:24–27) and by the Spirit (Acts 10:44–48). Frankly, I don't like when people interrupt me, but the Lord has interrupted me more than once and I'm glad He did!

If Peter had been thinking clearly and not been frightened, he would have realized several facts. First, Moses and Elijah were sent to encourage Jesus and not to remain on earth. Second, why would two men with homes in heaven want to live in huts on a mountaintop? What an insult! Third, Jesus was on His way to the cross and nothing could deter Him (Luke 9:51). Fourth, there was a desperate father at the base of the mountain with a demonized son and our Lord's disciples couldn't help him. (Of course, Peter didn't know this.) Alas, Peter still didn't understand the significance of the crucifixion (Matt. 16:21–23)! But let's not be too hard on Peter, because we're not too sure how we would have reacted had we been there, fighting sleep, and fearing an overshadowing cloud. Jesus came to the three frightened disciples, spoke to them, and touched them. That took care of everything!

At Christ's baptism, the Father had said, "This is My beloved Son, in whom I am well pleased" (Matt. 3:17), and He repeated those words on the mount, but He added, "Hear Him!" One of the most dangerous things we can do as disciples of the Lord Jesus is to tell the Lord what to do instead of letting Him tell us what to do. "For who has known the mind of the Lord? Or who has become His counselor?" (see Rom. 11:34, Isa. 40:13, and Jer. 23:18.) God doesn't need our advice, and when we give counsel to others, we had better know what we are saying. "To the law and to the testimony! If they do not speak according to this word, it is because there is no light in them" (Isa. 8:20). But Peter did get the message. Read and digest 2 Peter 1:12–21.

Jesus and the Father

This is the second time on record that the Father spoke from heaven to encourage the Son. He spoke at the baptism of Jesus, before Jesus went into the wilderness to be tempted by the devil; and the Father would speak again as Jesus drew near to His sacrifice on the cross (John 12:27–28). In each instance, the Father encouraged Jesus as He approached suffering and death. In our own walk with the Lord over many years, my wife and I have never faced a challenge or a crisis without receiving some word of encouragement from the Lord. Too many people wait for the crisis and then reach for their Bibles. The Lord has always given us our strengthening in the course of our personal daily Bible reading. We didn't find the promises, the promises found us!

Throughout His life and ministry on earth, Jesus and His Father worked together by the power of the Holy Spirit. The Father loves the Son (John 5:20), and loves us as He loves His Son (John 17:26); and as we walk in this loving relationship, we may experience the love, joy, and peace that the Spirit imparts in us and produces through us (Gal. 5:22).

Jesus Only

The heavenly visitors were gone and the three disciples saw "Jesus only." But that's all they needed to see! Moses and Elijah could do nothing for them—but Jesus could. There is no substitute for Jesus and no need to try to supplement Jesus with anyone or anything else. It's not Jesus plus Moses, because we are not saved by keeping the law (Gal. 2:16–21). It's not Jesus plus Elijah, for though he ministered to Israel, he cannot minister to us. It's not Jesus plus baptism, the Lord's Supper, or any other activity, because our religious works do not save us but only give evidence that we are saved.

There is no salvation without receiving Jesus by faith, and there is no satisfaction without loving and obeying Jesus day by day and seeking to glorify Him. *There is no true success in life without Jesus!* "He who abides in Me, and I in him, bears much fruit; for without Me you can do nothing" (John 15:5). It is "Jesus only" in our hearts, lives, and ministries—or it is nothing at all. Nothing!

"Jesus only" is not only the message of salvation and Christian living, but this is the key to understanding the Bible and growing in spiritual insight. There are dozens of study Bibles available today, but the key to a heart understanding any edition of Scripture is always Jesus. "And He opened their understanding that they night comprehend the Scriptures" (Luke 24:45).

> Beyond the sacred page
> I seek Thee, Lord.
> My spirit pants for Thee
> Thou living Word.

Those words by Mary A. Lathbury in the hymn "Break Thou the Bread of Life" have always meant much to me and have reminded me to seek the Lord Jesus Christ in the Bible and learn more about Him. (As a preacher and teacher, I tend to look for message outlines!) To read and study biblical history, biography, and even theology is not enough. We must see Jesus and learn more and more about Him.

Unless we make "Jesus only" the center of our lives, we can never enjoy the fullness of the Holy Spirit, for the Spirit was given to glorify Jesus (John 16:13–14). The Holy Spirit inspired people to write the Scriptures and to present Jesus Christ in what they wrote. It was a glorious day in my life when I learned that Jesus is found in the Old Testament as well as in the New Testament! I often urged the seminarians I was teaching to follow Paul's example and "preach Christ crucified" (1 Cor. 1:23) no matter what biblical text they were expounding. William Temple, Archbishop of Canterbury (1942–1944), said it so well: "Our message is Jesus Christ; we dare not give less and we cannot give more."

"Jesus only" is what gives power to our witnessing. I have friends who think that arguing theology and criticizing denominations is witnessing, but it's not. Getting people to agree with your denomination is not the same as telling people that Jesus *and only Jesus* is the Savior of the world. Our Lord didn't conduct a debate about Judaism vs. Samaritan religion when speaking to the woman at the well (John 4); He simply told her what she was missing and how she could get it. In our witnessing, we must use the Scriptures to present Christ and the cross, knowing that the gospel of Christ is "the power of God to salvation to everyone who believes" (Rom. 1:16).

"Jesus only" is the essential for effective prayer. To pray in the name of Jesus is to ask what He would ask so that He might be glorified, not so that we might be pacified. I have lived long enough to be thankful for unanswered prayer. We must pray for God's will to be done so that Jesus will be honored in all things (1 John 5:14–15), and the best way to determine God's will is to search the Scriptures and be taught by the Holy Spirit. Prayer becomes an adventure in faith as we grow in our communion with Jesus only.

Jesus and God's People Today

The word translated "transfigured" in Matthew 17:2 is used in two other places in the New Testament and is applied to believers today. You and I were not on the mount of transfiguration with Jesus, but we can have a metamorphosis experience in our own lives today. Yes, Jesus had a shining face, but so did Moses many centuries before (Exod. 34:29–30) and so did Stephen a few years after Jesus ascended to heaven (Acts 6:15). If you and I want to be transfigured and reveal the glory of God in a dark world, we must understand and obey the following four verses, which probably are familiar to you, but please read them carefully as if this were your first time. (I also suggest you read the third chapter of 2 Corinthians to see how Paul contrasts the old covenant glory and the new covenant glory.)

> I beseech you therefore, brethren [and this includes sisters], by the mercies of God, that you present your bodies a living sacrifice, holy, acceptable to God, which is your reasonable service. And do not be conformed to this world, but be transformed [transfigured] by the renewal of your mind, that you may prove what is that good and acceptable and perfect will of God. (Rom. 12:1–2)

> But we all, with unveiled face, beholding as in a mirror the glory of the Lord, are being transformed [transfigured] into the same image from glory to glory, just as by the Spirit of the Lord. (2 Cor. 3:18)

Five words summarize the essentials for the transfigured life. *Belonging.* "But we all" (2 Cor. 3:18) includes every Christian believer. The transfigured life isn't limited to prophets like Moses, apostles like Paul, or martyrs like Stephen. All true believers belong to God's family and therefore have the Holy Spirit within them and (I trust) the Holy Scriptures before them. Paul makes it clear that this glorious life is purely by the grace of God, for he contrasts the old covenant given by Moses with the new covenant established by Jesus. The old covenant was written on stones, but the new covenant is written on the believer's heart by the Holy Spirit. Christians are "living letters" that everybody may read (vv. 1–3). The old covenant law brought death but the new covenant gives us life (v. 6). The law cannot save us but instead condemns us, but the new covenant gives us righteousness and salvation (vv. 7–8). There was glory in the old covenant, but it faded away, while the new covenant glory grows "from glory to glory" (v. 18) until one day we will see Jesus and be like Him (1 John 3:1–3). Moses kept a veil on his face so the people would not see the glory fading, but believers today have nothing to hide because we have a perfect standing with the Lord (vv. 12–16; see Exod. 34:29–35). Today our unconverted Jewish friends have a veil over their hearts that prevents them from seeing the truth about Jesus. They are in bondage, but Christians enjoy freedom (vv. 15–17). So, if you belong to Jesus you may experience the transfiguration life!

Beseeching. This takes us to Romans 12:1–2 where the Lord tells us that, if we want the transfigured life, we must surrender ourselves completely to Him—body, mind, will, and heart. The renewing of our mind is an important part of the transfiguration process, for as we think, so we become. The word translated "beseech" also means "to exhort and appeal." God begs us to turn our lives over to Him because He knows what He has planned for us and what we will miss if we rebel. In the light of all the mercies He has showered upon us, explained in chapters 1–11, we ought to yield ourselves to Him and discover the joy of the "good and acceptable and perfect will of God." Just as the priests began each day at the altar, presenting a sacrifice to the Lord, so we should present ourselves as *living* sacrifices and, like Samuel, say, "Speak, Lord, for Your servant hears" (1 Sam. 3:9).

Believing. From start to finish, ours is a life of faith. It was faith in Jesus Christ that saved us (Eph. 2:8–9) and it is faith in Jesus Christ that enables us to know and do God's will as we serve Him. If we trust only in ourselves, we will receive only what we can do, but if we trust in the Lord and obey His will, we will receive every blessing He has planned for us *and we will be a blessing to others.* King David understood this and wrote in Psalm 31, "Oh, how great is Your goodness, which You have laid up for those who fear You, which You have prepared for those who trust in you" (v. 19). The Holy Spirit uses the word of God to strengthen our faith, because "faith comes by hearing, and hearing by the word of God" (Rom. 10:17).

Beholding (2 Cor. 3:18). The mirror is one of the many biblical symbols of the word of God (James 1:22–25). Unless we spend time each day looking into God's mirror and seeing the glory of Jesus, we can never experience the transfigured life. Most people spend time before a mirror daily, preparing themselves to look their best before they meet the outside world, and this is sensible. But it is also reasonable that we who follow Christ invest quality time looking into the Scriptures. We must realize that the Holy Spirit does not work in a vacuum but teaches us from the Scriptures and reveals Jesus to us. James tells us that the Scriptures are a mirror for *examination,* that we must take time to examine ourselves in light of what we read.

But if we stop with self-examination, we will probably be depressed; so the next step is *restoration.* The same word of God that reveals our sins will also help us experience the cleansing of our sins. "You are already clean because of the word which I have spoken to you," Jesus told His disciples (John 15:3), and Paul wrote that Christ desires to sanctify His church "with the washing of water by the word" (Eph. 5:26). "How can a young man cleanse his way?" asked the psalmist. "By taking heed according to Your word" (119:9).

But what connection is there between water and a mirror? I certainly don't wash my face in the mirror! Exodus 38:8 supplies the answer: the laver in the tabernacle was made from the brass mirrors of the Jewish women! They were melted down and molded into the laver where the priests washed their hands and feet. (There was no floor in the tabernacle.) Examination and restoration must be followed by transfiguration so that our clean faces radiate the glory of God. Wouldn't it be wonderful to have a mirror that removed all the soil and blemishes from your face? And let's thank God for 1 John 1:9! However, if we are wearing a mask, the mirror and the laver will do us no good. David found that out, didn't he (Ps. 32:3–5)?

Becoming. This is the result of our beholding: the better we see Jesus in the Scriptures and take it to heart, the more we become like Him, "transformed into the same image." If we do not make progress in the Christian life, we stand still and then begin to fall back. We should go from faith to faith (Rom. 1:17), grace to grace (John 1:16), strength to strength (Ps. 84:7), and glory to glory. We are transformed by the renewing of our mind (Rom. 12:2), and the Lord can then release His transforming power through us and accomplish His will on earth. It isn't enough just to pray "Your will be done on earth as it is in heaven" (Matt. 6:10). We must be available to do something about it! Too many professed Christians are conformers and not transformers (Rom. 12:2), and the Lord can't use them to make a difference in this needy world. I don't want to be a successful "comer" in this world; I want to be a successful "be-comer"—becoming more like Jesus "who went about doing good" (Acts 10:38).

(*The Milestone Mirror: A Pause for Reflection*)

The glory of God is a basic theme in the Bible. The prayer of Jesus recorded in John 17 has much to say about God's glory and God's people. Why?

How were Moses and Elijah connected with God's glory? How are you connected?

What is the relationship between prayer and God's glory? Like the three disciples, have you ever gone to sleep when you should have been praying?

What do you think of Peter's suggestion? How do we sometimes make the same mistake today?

6

The Triumphal Entry of Jesus

Matthew 21:1–11; Mark 11:1–11; Luke 19:28–44;
John 12:12–19

New York City has hosted some historic parades, three of which are known for the amount of ticker-tape that was used. In 1927 they welcomed Col. Charles Lindbergh home from his one-man non-stop flight to Paris, France, and 1,800 tons of paper fell on the parade route. For Gen. Douglas MacArthur's return in 1952, the number hit 3,249 tons; and for our first astronaut Col. John Glenn in 1962, the paper weighed in at 3,474 tons.

When Jesus entered Jerusalem on what the church calendar calls Palm Sunday, Matthew 21:10 tells us that "all the city was moved." The Greek word translated "moved" gives us the English word "seismograph," the instrument that measures the strength of earthquakes. Imagine, the arrival of Jesus in Jerusalem produced an emotional earthquake in the hearts and minds of the people, yet most of them rejected Him.

Jesus had often been in and out of Jerusalem, but His arrival that day was memorable because this time He had come to Jerusalem to die. "Now it came to pass, when the time had come for Him to be received up, that He steadfastly set His face to go to Jerusalem" (Luke 9:51). When Jesus died on the cross, a literal earthquake occurred (Matt. 27:50–51), and another one occurred at His tomb on resurrection morning—not to let Jesus out but to let His followers in to see that He was not there (Matt. 28:1–10). During His years of ministry, Jesus usually avoided actions that might lead to public controversy; but this time He made Himself the center of a parade as a last effort to reach His countrymen with the message of salvation. Let's examine the elements that made up this remarkable event and see what they say to us today.

Some Unidentified Disciples

For Jesus to fulfill the prophecy written in Zechariah 9:9, He needed a donkey with a colt. He sent two of His disciples to a nearby village, He told them what to do, and they came back with the donkey and the colt. The men in the village must have been believers who knew what Jesus was planning to do. We are not told when and how this was arranged, nor is it necessary for us to know. The main thing is this: when we obey the Lord's instructions, He takes care of working out the details. Later, Peter and John would have a similar experience when preparing the Passover supper (Luke 22:7–13).

There are many unnamed people in Scripture who faithfully served the Lord and have been rewarded accordingly. Who was the boy who gave his lunch to Jesus so He could feed that huge crowd? Who was the girl who suggested that her master Naaman go see the prophet and be cured of his leprosy (2 Kings 5)? What was the name of Paul's nephew who saved his uncle's life by revealing a plot to kill him? Does any Bible student know the name of the woman at Jacob's well who trusted Jesus and witnessed to the city (John 4)? It's not important that our names are recognized but that Jesus is glorified.

I think that some of our promotion of God's servants today is often displeasing to the Lord. Years ago in Melbourne, Australia, a church officer was excessively eloquent as he introduced the founder of the China Inland Mission, J. Hudson Taylor, climaxing with "our illustrious guest." Hudson Taylor stepped to the pulpit and said, "Dear friends, I am the little servant of an illustrious Master." If people go away from a worship service or a religious concert praising the participants instead of glorifying the Lord, we have failed and need to repent.

Two Unbroken Beasts

We must consider some interesting aspects of the provision of the animals. The first is that the men who were standing with the animals made no protest when the two disciples untied the beasts and began to lead them away. The problem was solved when the two disciples said, "The Lord has need of them." Those six simple monosyllables did the job and the disciples took the animals with them—and no doubt returned them when the event was over. As God's servants, we have no authority of our own but only the authority God gives us.

As I mentioned in a previous chapter, the Lord gave Adam and Eve dominion over creation (Gen. 1:26; Ps. 8:6–8), but they lost that privilege when they sinned. Jesus Christ, the Last Adam, has that dominion (Heb. 2:6–9; Rev. 1:5–6) and exercised it on that day. I would not want to ride a beast of burden that had not been broken, but Jesus was in perfect control. If we want to have peace of mind, we must remind ourselves frequently that God is in control and His timing is never wrong. "My times are in Your hands" (Ps. 31:15). If we are serving in His will and for His glory, we can be confident of His guidance, provision, and protection.

But most of all, how strange that the Creator and Lord of the universe should *need* something when He made and owns everything! "I will not take a bull from your house, nor goats out of your folds. For every beast of the forest is Mine, and the cattle on a thousand hills" (Ps. 50:9–10). When God made our first parents, He gave them the privilege of being His partners in the management of planet earth. We are fallen creatures today, but we are still responsible to the Lord for what we do with His creation. After God made the Garden of Eden, He needed some gardeners, so He enlisted Adam and Eve. When He wanted to build the nation of Israel, He called and blessed Abraham and Sarah and their descendants. When He needed a leader and deliverer for the Israelites, He drafted Moses; and when the nation invaded their Promised Land, He used Joshua to be their commander. The Lord is not only seeking the lost to save them, but He is also seeking for saved men and women who can serve Him (Ezek. 22:30).

Can God accomplish His will without our help? I think He can, but that isn't Plan 1. He enlists us, not because He needs us but because we need Him! As "God's fellow workers" (1 Cor. 3:9), we have the privilege of learning, growing, and sharing in the blessings of service. What an honor it is to know His will and do it! The Lord is searching for workers *for their sakes!* Each of us has a work to accomplish; to ignore it is to rob ourselves of God blessing and miss a future reward in heaven. Have you sought the Lord's will for your life? Have you been faithful to meet with the Lord daily and receive instructions?

An Unknowing Crowd

During the French revolution, a large crowd was seen running down a key avenue in Paris with a man frantically running several yards behind them. People on the sidewalk were shouting to the man, "Don't follow them! They're running right into trouble!" His reply was, "I have to follow them! I'm their leader!"

Sociologists tell us that they cannot predict what any one individual will do but that they can predict fairly accurately what crowds will do. Be it generated by fear, greed, hope, or selfishness, there is a "crowd mentality" that controls and unites people in crowds, whether or not they have a leader. The crowd on Palm Sunday was composed of Jerusalem citizens plus Jews and proselytes from other parts of the Holy Land and the Mediterranean world. The people who asked who Jesus was (Matt. 21:10) were visitors who had not heard about Him. There were people in the crowd who had witnessed the resurrection of Lazarus and they helped spread the word (John 12:17–18). We have no recorded words of Lazarus, but the people certainly talked a great deal about him! The fact that he was alive was a witness to our Lord's power and it moved many to believe in Him (John 12:9–11). It also moved the religious leaders to plot to kill both Jesus and Lazarus.

It's possible that this enthusiastic public demonstration had some political overtones, for some of the people were hoping that Jesus would free Israel from Roman bondage. The word "hosanna" that they cried means "save now," and it's unlikely they were all referring to a spiritual experience. It comes from Psalm 118:25–26: "Save now, I pray, O Lord; O Lord, I pray, send now prosperity. Blessed is he who comes in the name of the Lord." But Jesus "came to His own, and His own did not receive Him" (John 1:12). The psalmist predicted this: "The stone which the builders rejected has become the chief cornerstone" (118:22; cf. Matt. 21:40–42; Acts 4:11; 1 Peter 2:7).

Jesus had ministered for some three years, teaching in the synagogues and in the temple, doing miracles and preaching to the crowds, *yet the people were not sure who He was!* Some saw Him as the son of David or as a prophet (Matt. 21:9, 11). Had they known what Zechariah wrote about Him, they would have known He was their King (Matt. 21:5; Zech. 9:9). The priests and scribes who claimed to know the Scriptures should have identified Him early in His public ministry, but they persisted in their ignorance. But is the spiritual perception of the crowd any better today? I fear not. The people in Jesus' day could gather together at Passover for a religious feast *and yet reject the very Lamb of God who was in their midst!*

When you read Zechariah 9:1–10, you see a contrast between two rulers: Alexander the Great (vv. 1–8) and Jesus (vv. 9–10). The prophet describes the conquests of Alexander, who was a leader whose goal was to rule the world, and then he describes Jesus, the true King of Israel and the King of Kings. Alexander was proud, while Jesus was gentle and humble, riding a lowly donkey. Alexander brought fear and bondage to the nations, while Jesus brings us joy and freedom. Jesus was just, but Alexander was a law unto himself. Alexander brought death to multitudes, while Jesus imparts eternal life and peace to all who trust Him. Jesus said, "I have come that they may have life, and that they may have it more abundantly" (John 10:10). Alexander's conquests did not last, but the life that Jesus gives us is eternal.

Many Unexpected Tears

If you and I had been acclaimed as Jesus was that day, we probably would have ended the occasion with a speech and gained even more recognition; but Jesus beheld the city and wept over it. A short time before, He had wept quietly at the grave of Lazarus (John 11:35), but this time He wept aloud at the ignorance and unbelief of the city (Luke 19:41–45). Some of the people had shouted, "Blessed be the King who comes in the name of the Lord. Peace in heaven and glory in the highest" (Luke 19:38). At Christ's birth, the angels had announced "peace on earth" (Luke 2:13–14), but Jesus had announced war on earth (Luke 12:49–51). The only way to enjoy peace is in the will of God, and Jesus had been rejected by the leaders. They did not know the time of their visitation—that the Messiah had been with them and had offered them peace—but they declared war (Luke 19:41–44). No wonder He wept!

The chief priests and the elders confronted Jesus after the triumphal entry and questioned His authority to cleanse the temple (Matt. 21:12–17, 23–27). He silenced them by asking one question, and then told three parables that exposed their disobedience and ignorance. Then He made an announcement that sealed their judgment: "Therefore I say to you, the kingdom of God will be taken from you and given to a nation bearing the fruits of it" (Matt. 21:43). That "nation" is the church, "a chosen generation, a royal priesthood, a holy nation, His own special people" (1 Peter 2:9). Some of the titles that the Lord had given to Israel were now given to the church.

Our Lord knew that the city of Jerusalem was destined to be captured by the Roman army, the temple and city destroyed, and many people killed. His prophecy was fulfilled in AD 70. Jesus began His public ministry about AD 30, which means that the nation was given some forty years to repent and turn to the Lord. That's how many years their ancestors were given when they marched from Sinai to the Promised Land. That journey could have been accomplished in eleven days (Deut. 1:2), but the nation's unbelief and rebellion turned it into a journey of thirty-eight years (Deut. 2:14). Such are the consequences of unbelief.

During His earthly ministry, Jesus never sought for the praises of men as the Pharisees did (Matt. 6:5–6; 23:1–12). He sought only to please the Father (John 8:29). He sometimes told the people whom He had healed not to tell others who did it, and He sometimes went into the wilderness alone to avoid the crowds. Had Israel's religious leaders listened to Christ's teaching, studied their own Scriptures, and trusted their Messiah, their future would have been different. "The Lord is . . . not willing that any should perish but that all should come to repentance" (2 Peter 3:9). "How often I wanted to gather your children together . . . but you were not willing" (Matt. 23:37).

Our Lord was not impressed with the crowd's enthusiastic praise. Instead, He wept over Jerusalem (Matt. 23:37–39), for He knew that the judgment of the Lord was coming.

(*The Milestone Mirror: A Pause for Reflection*)

Some people get upset if their names are left out of the "thank you" column in the church bulletin, while others get upset if their names *are* included! Does it upset or anger you if you are not recognized and thanked? Do you enjoy compliments?

Are you impressed by so-called famous people? Why? Does admiring them help you live a more satisfying Christian life?

Jesus rode into the city to fulfill the prophecy in Zechariah 9:9. We are safe if what we do is authorized by Scripture. Do you test your thoughts, plans, and deeds by what the Bible says?

Have you ever heard speakers talk more about themselves than about Jesus Christ? How did you respond? I have heard sermons in which Jesus was never mentioned! The Holy Spirit wants to help us glorify Jesus (John 16:14).

Do you feel that the size of the crowd is a valid measure of the success of a gathering? Have you noticed that Dr. Luke mentions the size of the Jerusalem church early in the book of Acts (1:15; 2:41; 4:4) and then drops crowd statistics altogether?

7

The Arrest of Jesus in the Garden

Matthew 26:36–56; Mark 14:32–42; Luke 22:31–53;
John 18:1–11

The Jewish priests and elders sent a large band of armed people to arrest Jesus and bring Him before the official Jewish council to be tried. The council had already determined that He was guilty and must be killed. Judas the traitor, the thieving treasurer of the twelve apostles (John 12:1–8), led the way to the garden. But this biblical record of the arrest of the Master is much more than an account of an evil deed, for it is rich in images that reveal the sinfulness of man and the graciousness of God.

The Garden

Human history began in a garden (Gen. 2:8–25), and for those who have trusted Christ, life will be eternally blessed in the glorious garden city that Jesus and Paul called "Paradise" (Luke 23:43; 2 Cor. 12:4, and see Rev. 21–22). Jesus frequently met with His disciples in the garden of Gethsemane on the slope of the Mount of Olives (Luke 22:39), and it was there He taught them and prayed with them. The name "Gethsemane" means "oil press" because there were many olive trees there.

Besides being a food, olives were important to the life of the people in the ancient Near East because the oil was used for cooking; personal hygiene; medication; fuel for lamps; the anointing of prophets, priests, and kings; and the offering of sacrifices. It was known as "the oil of gladness" (Ps. 45:7; Isa. 61:3), and to have an abundance of oil and wine was a mark of prosperity. The olives had to be crushed between two large heavy rocks in the oil press, a symbol of personal suffering. This reminds us that, though life has its times of affliction, the Lord can bring something good out of what appears to be bad. First the crushing and then the blessing.

The Cup

Jesus led His disciples into Gethsemane and left eight of them together near the entrance while He took Peter, James, and John with Him farther into the garden. There He prayed three times, "O My Father, if it is possible, let this cup pass from Me; nevertheless, not as I will, but as You will" (Matt. 26:39, 42, 44). In Scripture, drinking a cup symbolizes obediently accepting the will of God, even if it involves sacrifice and pain. When the Father sends us blessing and our cup runs over (Pss. 16:5–6; 23:5), we gladly drink it; but He may hand us a bitter cup of chastening to drink (Pss. 73:10; 102:9). The cup Jesus would drink on the cross would be more than physical pain, for on the cross He would bear the judgment of the sins of the world (1 Peter 2:24). He would be made sin for us (2 Cor. 5:21), be made a curse for us (Gal. 3:13), and be forsaken by the Father (Matt. 27:46). This was this "cup" about which the Master was praying.

But our Lord did not hesitate to take the cup, nor should we, because each cup is prepared lovingly by the Father and suited to our needs. If I can sincerely say, "I delight to do Your will, O my God, and Your law is in my heart" (Ps. 40:8), then receiving the cup and drinking it will glorify God and edify me; but if I resist, I will grieve the Lord and rob myself of the blessing the Lord had prepared for me. The Father knows exactly what we need, how much we need, and when we need to receive it; He never makes a mistake. In our unbelief, we sometimes think that we are drowning in suffering (Ps. 130), when actually God ministers to us a cup at a time. We must follow Christ's example when He rebuked Peter for using his sword: "Shall I not drink the cup which My Father has given me?" (John 18:11).

The Sleepers

Three times our Lord paused in His praying and went to see if Peter, James, and John were praying also, only to find them sleeping. You will recall that He had a similar experience with these men on the mount of transfiguration (Luke 10:32). While they were sleeping in the garden, Jesus was praying with such fervor that His sweat fell to the ground like drops of blood! The Father sent an angel to strengthen Him (Luke 22:41–44), yet a few hours later, Peter would be standing by the enemy's fire to keep warm! Jesus was sweating but Peter was shivering. Is there a spiritual lesson here?

Our Lord's loving rebuke is good counsel for us today: "Watch and pray, lest you enter into temptation. The spirit indeed is willing, but the flesh is weak" (Matt. 26:41). When it comes to sinning, the flesh is strong; but when it comes to godly living, "the flesh profits nothing" (John 6:63). The first time you find the phrase "watch and pray" in Scripture is in Nehemiah 4:9: "we made our prayer to our God, and . . . we set a watch against them day and night." Watching means keeping awake and being alert, and praying means trusting God to help us defeat the enemy. The prophet Isaiah said that Israel's spiritual leaders in his day were like watchmen that could not see and watchdogs that could not bark (Isa. 56:10). Talk about uselessness!

There is such a thing as a "carnal stupor" that puts undisciplined Christians into a spirit of lethargy. Jesus called the church at Laodicea "lukewarm"; He wished that the people were either hot or cold and therefore conscious of their need (Rev. 3:14–19). Paul warned the believers in Rome to "awake out of sleep" (13:11) and to get up, dress up, and stand up for the battle (Rom. 13:11–14). Christian soldiers must not attempt to walk or make war in their sleep! In Mark 13, Jesus describes the spiritual condition in the end times, and closes with, "Take heed, watch and pray" (v. 33). That is how to have victory over *the world*. "Watch and pray" also helps to give us victory over the *flesh* (Mark 14:38) and also over the *devil* (Eph. 6:18). "Continue earnestly in prayer, being vigilant in it with thanksgiving," Paul admonished the Colossian believers, for then God will open doors of ministry and overcome the adversaries (4:2–4). "Therefore let us not sleep, as others do, but let us watch and be sober" (1 Thess. 6–11). There is no place in God's church for sleepwalkers. "Awake to righteousness, and do not sin" (1 Cor. 15:34).

The Kiss

Kissing is almost universally understood as an expression of affection, whether that affection is based on kinship, friendship, romance, or discipleship. Family members kissed each other and the Jewish rabbi was usually kissed by his students. When Paul told his friends they would not see his face again, they wept and kissed him affectionately (Acts 20:37–38). In the western world the men usually shake hands, but in the biblical world they kissed one another. However, not all the kisses found in Scripture are what Paul called "a holy kiss" (Rom. 16:16; 1 Cor. 16:20; 2 Cor. 13:12; 1 Tim. 5:26). Masquerading as his brother Esau, Jacob kissed his father Isaac and received the family blessing (Gen. 27:26–29). Absalom gave counterfeit kisses to one and all and captured his father David's crown (2 Sam. 15), and Joab used a kiss to cover his murdering of Amasa (2 Sam. 20). But the foulest desecration of the kiss occurred in Gethsemane the night Judas led a mob into the garden and identified Jesus by kissing Him. Jesus said, "Judas, are you betraying the Son of Man with a kiss?" (Luke 22:48).

In the streets, synagogues, and temple courts, Jesus had been quite visible for three years, so it's remarkable that Judas had to point Him out at all. But it was night and Jesus was known as a miracle worker, so Judas didn't take any chances. When Judas kissed Him, did Proverbs 27:6 come to our Lord's mind? "Faithful are the wounds of a friend, but the kisses of an enemy are deceitful." The wounds of Jesus purchased our redemption, but the kisses of Judas sealed his own condemnation.

Judas was an apostle of Jesus Christ and the treasurer of the disciple band, but he had never been born again (John 6:63–71). We must remember that Judas was finally controlled by the devil (John 13:2, 26–27). Judas had never believed in Jesus as his own personal Lord and Savior (John 13:11, 18). Why, then, did he accept the call Jesus gave him to become one of His followers? Jesus knew that Judas would betray Him, yet He chose Him and to the very end protected Him. Had Peter known that Judas left the upper room to betray Jesus to the elders and chief priests, he might have drawn his sword earlier!

There is a theory, which I do not endorse, that Judas thought Jesus would remove the Romans and re-establish the Jewish kingdom, and he wanted to support Him. After all, he might be named treasurer of the kingdom! But some of the other disciples nurtured that same kingdom hope. James and John had their mother ask Jesus for special thrones in the kingdom (Matt. 20:20–28), and the twelve often discussed which of them was the greatest in the kingdom (Luke 9:46–48; 22:24). Even after our Lord's resurrection, the apostles still asked if He would now restore the kingdom to Israel (Acts 1:6–8). The theory claims that Judas thought that by creating a crisis he would force Jesus to use His powers to defeat the Romans and bring in the kingdom. Instead, our Lord submitted to the Jews and the Romans and went to the cross to die. Judas did not really know the Master. The deceitfulness of riches had choked the seed Jesus had planted in his heart (Matt. 13:22). "For the love of money is a root of all kinds of evil" (1 Tim. 6:10).

Jesus called Judas "the son of perdition" (John 17:12), which can be translated "son of lostness." Judas stole money from the disciples' treasury and received money from the priests, but in the end, he lost everything. He ruined a good name—Judah, which means praise. He lost his character as he lied, robbed the treasury, and conspired with the enemy; and he lost opportunities to yield to the Savior. Judas was a child of the devil—a liar and a murderer (John 8:44).

But I fear there are Judases in our churches today, counterfeit Christians who have never put their trust in Jesus Christ. Judas heard Jesus teach and preach, he saw Him perform miracles, and yet he rejected Him. How close Judas was to experiencing salvation and yet rejected it! This reminds me of some of the closing words of John Bunyan's *The Pilgrim's Progress, Part 1:* "Then I saw that there was a way to hell, even from the gates of heaven." So near and yet so far!

When I think of Judas Iscariot, I think of Proverbs 23:23: "Buy the truth and do not sell it." Jesus is the truth, and the other apostles gave up everything to follow Him. Judas sold the truth for the price of a slave. The names of the other apostles are written for eternity on the twelve foundations of the walls of the new Jerusalem (Rev. 21:9–14). Judas is not there. His name is written in the dictionary I just consulted as the man who betrayed Jesus. His name is also found in my thesaurus under "traitor."

The Sword

Of all the apostles, I think Peter is my favorite, probably because I painfully identify with his impatience and his tendency to get his exercise by jumping to conclusions. I am not worthy to carry Peter's sandals, and I don't like it when my fellow preachers ridicule him for his mistakes as if they had never failed the Lord. When Jesus first told the twelve He would be arrested and crucified, Peter took Him aside and said, "Far be it from You, Lord; this shall not happen to You" (Matt. 16:21–23). Imagine giving orders to the Lord, but I fear we have all done it.

Jesus took the cup and obeyed the Father's will, Judas rejected God's will, but Peter with his sword also resisted God's will. If Jesus had wanted protection or deliverance, He could have asked the Father for more than twelve legions of angels—six thousand angels for Him and six thousand for each of the eleven men with Him (Matt. 26:53). But those seventy-two thousand heavenly soldiers were not needed, for the Master had the best protection available—He was doing the will of the Father.

On their way to the garden, Jesus spoke to the men about swords, but Peter failed to get the message (Luke 22:35–38). Jesus reminded them that He had always cared for them as they had all ministered together. However, with His death on the cross, their circumstances would change and now they had to be prepared for opposition. The disciples took His words literally and assured Him that they were adequately equipped with two swords. Peter had one of them.

We need to understand that Peter got into trouble because he was not rightly related to the word of God and the will of God. The record is in Luke 22:31–62. First, Peter argued with the word and boasted that he was ready to meet the enemy and give his life for Jesus (vv. 31–34). Peter thought he knew himself but he did not, and instead of defending Jesus, he denied Jesus. The people who say, "Well, if I know my own heart" had better read Jeremiah 17:9. Then Peter misinterpreted the word of God and thought that Jesus had commanded them to use their swords (vv. 35–38). His third blunder was to disobey the word and go to sleep when he should have been praying (vv. 39–46). Peter went to sleep on the mount of transfiguration and almost missed seeing and hearing Moses and Elijah. In the garden he did miss seeing the angel come from heaven and strengthen Jesus.

Then Peter ran ahead of God's word and almost killed a man (vv. 47–53). When the mob appeared, the apostles asked, "Lord, shall we strike with the sword?" but did not wait for an answer. Peter did everything wrong. He fought the wrong enemy (Eph. 6:10–12) with the wrong energy (John 6:63) and using the wrong equipment (2 Cor. 10:3–6; Heb. 4:12; Eph. 6:17). Along with all these mistakes, Peter was motivated by the wrong purpose: he was trying to deliver Jesus! "Put your sword into the sheath," Jesus commanded Peter. "Shall I not drink the cup which the Father has given Me?" (John 18:11). But Jesus forgave Peter and used him mightily. At Pentecost, Peter would wield the sword of the Spirit and "slay" three thousand men!

Peter climaxed this zealous disobedience by following Jesus to the high priest's house when Jesus had told the disciples to scatter (John 16:32). I have heard sermons that criticized Peter for "following at a distance" (Matt. 26:58), *but he was not supposed to follow at all!* In the upper room Jesus quoted Zechariah 13:7, "Strike the Shepherd, and the sheep will be scattered" (Matt. 26:31), and He said to those apprehending Him, "Therefore if you seek Me, let these go their way" (John 18:8). Jesus made it clear that the men were supposed to get out of the garden immediately. Had Peter obeyed, he probably would not have denied the Lord three times. Each of us must decide if we will go through life wielding the sword or drinking the cup. Yes, there are times when physical defense and legal measures are legitimate; we see this in the ministry of Paul (Acts 16:35–40; 22:22–29). But if I am always carrying the sword and fighting the enemy in my own strength, it will be difficult to drink the cup and obey God's will.

How gracious the Lord was at that critical moment when He healed Malchus's ear! Jesus rebuked Peter and repaired the damage even though neither Peter nor Malchus deserved it. Had He not done so, the officers might well have arrested Peter! Even so, Peter's impulsive deed almost got him into trouble while he was warming himself at the fire in the high priest's courtyard, for a relative of Malchus saw what Peter did in the garden and asked him about it (John 18:25–30). Did our Lord's healing of the ear touch the heart of Malchus? Did Peter and Malchus ever meet during those exciting days recorded in Acts 1–12? Did Malchus ever receive Christ? We don't know the answers, but we trust that Malchus got the message.

Jesus compared Himself to a physician and lost sinners to sick patients (Matt. 9:9–13). He healed the bodies of many sick people and even raised the dead, and all of this was a vivid demonstration of the spiritual healing He can bring to our lives. We live in a world that has rejected Jesus and yet we must continue to invite "sick sinners" to come to the Great Physician, trust Him, and be healed in their hearts. Jesus makes house calls *and He has already paid the bill!* Jesus taught us to forgive our enemies and to do them good (Matt. 5:41–48), and He dramatically demonstrated this love in the garden and on the cross. "Father, forgive them, for they do not know what they do" (Luke 23:34).

You and I don't carry swords and cut off people's ears, but we do have tongues that can be used like swords and do all sorts of damage *through* people's ears. How easy it is to get angry and make cutting remarks that pain the heart. "There is one who speaks like the piercings of the sword, but the tongue of the wise promotes health" (Prov. 12:18). We can start arguments or share gossip that will spread like a forest fire and do almost irreparable damage (James 3:5–6). During World War II, you may have seen the posters that read "Loose lips sink ships." Loose lips can also damage families, destroy marriages, and divide churches. There is great power in the tongue. I am told that for every word in Adolf Hitler's book *Mein Kampf* ("my fight") 127 people died in World War II. "Death and life are in the power of the tongue," wrote Solomon (Prov. 18:21), and we make the choice. May we go through life building, not destroying; and bringing health and healing to others, not pain.

(*The Milestone Mirror: A Pause for Reflection*)

Jesus had a private place in the garden of Gethsemane where He and His disciples could meet and not be disturbed. There He taught them and there they prayed. Do you have a "holy of holies" where you live, whether at home or on the college or university campus? Do you get alone with the Lord daily and meditate on the Scriptures and pray? Our daily meeting with the Lord is one of the essentials of a fruitful Christian life. "What, could you not watch with Me one hour?" our Lord asked Peter, James, and John (Matt. 26:40). How would you answer?

Just as the hypocrite Judas invaded the garden, so Satan wants to invade our daily meeting with the Lord. As we are meditating on Scripture or praying, we remember things we must do or things we did we should not have done. Our mind wanders and sometimes our thoughts are not spiritual. I have learned that the "invaders" are usually things in my life I have not seriously turned over to the Lord. How do you deal with your "invaders"?

When the enemy attacks, do you surrender to the Father as Jesus did, or do you try to fight in your own strength as Peter did? Remember the prayer of our Lord: "O My Father, not as I will, but as You will" (John 26:39). I have fought some difficult battles in my prayer time, and the victory always came when I surrendered everything to God's will.

8

The Trial and Rejection of Jesus

Matthew 26:57–27:31; Mark 14:53–15:20;
Luke 22:54–23:25; John 18:12–19:16

According to *The American Heritage Dictionary,* a legal trial is "the examination of evidence and applicable law by a competent tribunal to determine the issue of specified charges and claims." If that definition applies to trials in ancient Israel, then neither the Jewish trial of Jesus nor the Roman trial was legal.

Jesus appeared before the chief priests and scribes and was "tried" because He claimed to be the Son of God. To the Jewish Sanhedrin, this claim was blasphemy, and they had already decided that Jesus must die. He was also examined by Pontius Pilate, the Roman governor, who was told by the Jews that Jesus claimed to be a king. "We have no king but Caesar!" the crowd shouted, but Pilate knew how much the Jews despised the Romans, especially the governor. The governor questioned Jesus and announced that he found no reason why He should to die; but the voices of the Jewish mob prevailed. Finally, Pilate washed his hands of the matter and, to please the Jewish mob, released the notorious prisoner Barabbas and condemned Jesus to be crucified.

Let's learn what we can from what the key persons did in those so-called trials.

Conspiracy:
Judas Went Out and Bargained with the Scribes and Chief Priests

At the last supper with His disciples, Jesus gave Judas the morsel of bread and said to him, "'What you do, do quickly.'. . . Having received the piece of bread, he went out immediately. And it was night" (John 13:27, 30). I might add that it is still night for Judas and always will be night. When Jesus was arrested, He said to the officers, "But this is your hour, and the power of darkness" (Luke 22:53). Judas bargained with the chief priests for thirty pieces of silver, which they probably paid him after Jesus was arrested (Matt. 26:14–16), and which he gave back to them before he went out and hanged himself (Matt. 27:3–10).

The first mention of the Jewish council's decision to kill Jesus occurred after Jesus had healed a man in a synagogue after a Sabbath service (Matt. 12:9–14.) To the religious leaders, healing on the Sabbath was defiling the Sabbath, and from that time on, the priests and scribes waited for a convenient time to arrest Jesus. In fact, it became common knowledge that they wanted to kill Him. (See John 5:18; 7:1, 19, 25; 8:37; 11:16, 47–57; and 12:19.)

The religious leadership of the Jewish people was at a very low level. They had two high priests, Caiaphas and his father-in-law Annas. And Caiaphas was a Sadducee. He did not believe in the resurrection of the human body or the existence of angels and spirits. When they brought Jesus to Pilate, the leaders refused to enter the Roman government building lest they be defiled by the pagan Gentiles. Maintaining the traditions of a holy day was more important to them than speaking the truth or giving an innocent prisoner a fair trial (John 18:28).

But Pilate knew that the religious leaders wanted to destroy Jesus because they were envious of Him—His popularity with the people, His amazing miracles, and His knowledge of God's word (Matt. 27:18). No matter how carefully they watched Jesus or how cleverly they questioned Him, they could find nothing to condemn; and if they did arrest Him, they feared creating an uproar among the people. The priests and scribes therefore were pleased when Judas turned traitor and solved their problems. Jesus was first taken to Caiaphas and then to Annas, the father-in-law of Caiaphas, where the soldiers abused Him before He was then returned to Annas.

How sad it was for God's chosen people Israel to have such un-spiritual religious leaders, but from the beginning of the official Jewish priesthood, there were leaders who sinned. The first high priest was Aaron and his two sons Nadab and Abihu were killed by the Lord because they rushed into the tabernacle with false fire (Lev. 10). During the reign of Ahaz, the king visited Damascus and saw a pagan altar he admired; so he commanded Uriah the high priest to make a duplicate. In defiance of God's word, Uriah obeyed and put the new altar in the temple and the true altar dedicated to the Lord was shoved aside (2 Kings 16:10–15). In the days of Nehemiah, Eliashib the priest allowed Tobiah, the ene-my of Israel, to use one of the temple storerooms (Neh. 13:4–14). When Nehemiah discovered it, he threw out both Tobiah and his personal belongings and restored the room for the use of the Lord's people. Nehemiah also dealt with the son of one of the priests who had married a pagan wife (Neh. 13:23–29). When you read the first two chapters of Malachi, you see how unfaith-ful the priests were and how their sins hindered the Lord who wanted to bless His people.

But before we condemn the ancient Israelites, let's examine today's churches and see how obedient we are in our work. What kind of people are permitted to use facilities dedicated to the ser-vice of the Lord? Is the "spiritual furniture" built according to the Lord's blueprints or the blueprints dreamed up by the worldly crowd? Like King Ahaz, are we getting our plans from the world and are they better than the plans that the Lord provides? God warned Moses, "And you shall raise up the tabernacle according to its pattern you were shown on the mount" (Exod. 26:30; and see Exod. 25:40 and 39:42–43, as well as Acts 7:44 and Heb. 8:5). When the Lord repeats a truth that many times, we had better pay attention.

When they arrested Jesus, it appeared to be the beginning of success; but He said to them, "But this is your hour, and the power of darkness" (Luke 22:53). Anything against God managed by Satan will ultimately fail. The conspiracy was temporarily successful and the council voted to request the Roman officials to have Jesus crucified. It looked as though the prince of darkness was winning, but he was not. Calvary was victory and not defeat, for on the cross Jesus "disarmed principalities and powers [and] made a public spectacle of them, triumphing over them in it [the cross]." Martin Luther said it like this:

> The prince of darkness grim—
> We tremble not for him;
> His rage we can endure,
> For lo! His doom is sure,
> One little word shall fell him.

Compromise:
Pontius Pilate Went in and out, Looking for a Loophole

The one thing the Romans demanded of their local governors was that they maintain peace and unity among their subjects. This was for the good of the empire, the glory of the emperor, and the protection of the governor's job. But with thousands of visitors from many lands in Jerusalem at Passover season, anything was liable to happen. Pilate was awakened early in the morning to deal with a Jewish delegation about a case of capital punishment—Jesus of Nazareth. The delegation would not enter the governor's building lest they be defiled by the Gentiles and unable to participate in Passover; so Pilate went out to meet them. When you read John 18:29–19:16, you find Pilate making at least seven different moves, going out and coming in, and each time he tried to avoid making a decision about Jesus. Statesmen do the right thing; politicians do the safe thing.

The priests and scribes knew they could not influence Pilate if they talked about theology, so they charged Jesus with being a political trouble maker. "We found this fellow perverting the nation, and forbidding to pay taxes to Caesar, saying that He Himself is Christ, a king" (Luke 23:2). The three words "taxes," "Caesar," and "king" would get the governor's attention immediately. Their statement about Caesar and taxes was a lie (see Luke 22:15–22), and Jesus was not the kind of king Caesar was accustomed to fear. When Pilate questioned Jesus, he asked what kind of a kingdom He ruled, and the Lord made it clear that His kingdom was spiritual and personal and not political or of this world. Our Lord was not like a Roman dictator or even like one of the rulers in the Herodian dynasty of that day (John 18:36–37; see John 17:6, 11, 16). Pilate was shocked that Jesus did not reply to the accusations of the priests and scribes, nor did He always reply to Pilate. Jesus was in the will of God and had nothing to fear from priests or politicians.

When Pilate learned that Jesus came from Galilee, he was sure he had found a loophole, so he sent Jesus to Herod Antipas, the man who had killed John the Baptist (Luke 23:7–12). Herod was delighted to see Jesus, not because he wanted spiritual help but because he was hoping to be entertained by one of our Lord's miracles. He asked Jesus many questions, but the Lord remained silent. God had sent John the Baptist to warn Herod about his sinful life and Herod had killed him to please his unlawful wife and her daughter, both of whom hated John (Mark 6:14–29). When Herod killed John, he silenced the voice of God, and that is why Jesus said nothing to him. Herod's men mocked Jesus and put a gorgeous robe on Him and sent Him back to Pilate; but the transaction reunited Herod and Pilate, mending their broken friendship. The world is united in loving sin and hating Jesus and those who belong to Him.

Pilate tried another stratagem. He told the Jewish priests and rulers that he had not found Jesus guilty of any capital crime, nor had King Herod. The governor reminded them of the Roman custom of releasing one prisoner at Passover, and he gave them the choice of Jesus or a notorious prisoner named Barabbas, who was a murderer and an insurrectionist. Pilate knew neither the ignorance of the crowd nor the influence of the Jewish leaders who prompted them, because the people shouted for Barabbas. (By the way, this is not the same crowd that shouted "hosanna" on Palm Sunday. This crowd was controlled by the religious leaders.) The mob voted for Barabbas!

Pilate then had Jesus scourged with whips embedded with pieces of metal and bone, a terrible punishment; and the Roman soldiers dressed Him in a robe and put a crown of thorns on His head. Appealing to the pity of the crowd, Pilate presented "king Jesus" to them, but they only cried louder for Barabbas! The governor declared Jesus innocent and sought to release Him (John 19:12), but the crowd responded by crying out, "Crucify Him! Crucify Him!" The world chooses the guilty criminal and rejects the innocent Redeemer. The world has not changed.

When it comes to deciding to follow Christ, there is no place for compromise. Unfortunately, Pilate learned that truth too late, if he learned it at all. Judas pleased himself by betraying Jesus and Pilate pleased the people (Mark 15:15) by cooperating with them in their evil desires. Pilate the man faced a choice and could not avoid Jesus no matter how he tried. Pilate the governor fought his conscience and tried every device to wash his hands of Jesus, but he failed. He went in and out, questioning Jesus and hearing the crowd. He decided that it was best to "take the easy way" and it turned out to be the worst way.

Revelation 21:8 lists the kinds of unsaved people who end up in the lake of fire.

First on the list is "the cowardly."

Compassion:
"So They Took Jesus and Led Him Away" (John 19:16)

Judas was involved in a conspiracy and went out "and it was night" (John 19:30). Pilate was looking for a compromise and went in and out, hoping to find a peaceful solution to his dilemma. As we now meditate on the solemn and crucial event of our Lord's march to the cross, let's set aside the traditions that are not supported by the inspired Scriptures. Instead, let's embrace the facts found in the record, searching for the spiritual truths behind these facts and taking them to heart.

The so-called trials were now ended, Jesus had been declared guilty, and the soldiers led Him out of the Roman Praetorium to the place called Calvary. "He was led as a lamb to the slaughter" (Isa. 53:7). He began his march at the Praetorium, carrying on His shoulder the cross on which He would die (John 19:17). By carrying the heavy piece of wood, He was announcing to everyone that He, Jesus of Nazareth, was a guilty criminal! Of course, it was a lie.

But then a remarkable thing happened. No sooner did the procession leave the Roman Praetorium than the soldiers conscripted Simon of Cyrene to carry the cross (Luke 23:26)! Roman soldiers had the authority to "draft" citizens for useful work (Matt. 5:41), but the choice of Simon was not a mere coincidence.

Simon had traveled some 800 miles to get to Jerusalem for Passover and had lodged out in the country a few miles from the city. He had no idea when he walked through the Jerusalem gate that he would be involved in a crucial event that would be written about and discussed around the world for centuries to come. But the important thing is this: Jesus did not carry His cross publicly from the Praetorium to Golgotha *because He was not guilty!* He was the spotless Lamb of God who would give His life for our salvation.

Believers today cannot literally carry Christ's cross day after day and night after night, but we *can* carry a cross for Christ. True discipleship is much more than studying the Bible, praying, and meeting with other believers. True discipleship means public identification with Jesus, "the fellowship of His sufferings" (Phil. 3:10) and the willingness to die for what He has willed for us. "Follow Me, and I will make you fishers of men" (Matt. 4:19). "If anyone desires to come after Me," said Jesus, "let him deny himself, and take up his cross and follow Me" (Matt. 10:24).

But back to Simon of Cyrene. How does he fit into this narrative? You will recall that Simon Peter boasted that he was ready to go to prison and to death for Jesus' sake, but Peter was nowhere to be seen as Jesus went to Calvary. Simon Peter was replaced by an unknown visitor from a distant land, Simon from Cyrene. Mark 15:21 tells us that Simon of Cyrene was "the father of Alexander and Rufus," believers who were known and appreciated in the early church; and in Romans 16:13, Paul greets a believer named Rufus, whose mother had ministered to the apostle in some special way. Simon not only *carried* the cross for Jesus, but also *trusted* in the Savior and went home and led his wife and sons to faith in Christ. The family became well known to the churches. What began as a humiliating experience for Simon ended up a great blessing for him, his family, and other believers—even today! Only God can turn a curse into a blessing (Deut. 23:5; Neh. 13:2).

Luke tells us that a great crowd was following the procession going to Calvary, among them a group of women who were weeping (23:27–31). They are not identified as believers but were probably women who wanted to encourage the condemned victims. Not everyone in the city was heartless. Luke was a doctor with a sympathetic heart. When you read his Gospel, notice how often he mentions women. Jesus heard them weeping and paused to speak to them. His basic message was, "Don't weep for Me. I'm doing My Father's will. Weep for yourselves and for your children, because terrible judgment is coming to the city of Jerusalem."

The image of green wood and dry wood comes from an ancient popular saying to which Jesus gave a prophetic meaning. During our Lord's three years of public ministry, Israel was especially blessed. But Israel's leaders rejected the Son of God and asked to have Him killed. If the Lord allowed His innocent Son (the green tree) to be killed, what will He do to those who were guilty of the great sin of rejecting Him and having Him crucified? The Jewish nation was like a dry tree that deserved to be burned up. Some forty years later, Titus and the Roman army fulfilled that prophecy when they attacked Jerusalem, and many women and children suffered severely. In Luke 13:34–35 and 19:41–44, our Lord had already spoken of this coming judgment.

Judas pleased himself and lost everything. Pilate pleased the people and crucified the Son of God. Jesus always did what pleased the Father (John 8:29) and brought salvation. The world rejects Jesus and asks for Barabbas. The world rejects those who follow Jesus (John 17:14), but He is with us and will ultimately give us the victory.

(The Milestone Mirror: A Pause for Reflection)

Jesus knew what the Father wanted Him to do, and He did it. He was humiliated, whipped, and crucified, and He paid the price of our salvation. Do you thank Him for that? Do you thank Him often or just when you participate in the Lord's Supper? Paul gloried in the cross (Gal. 6:14) and so should we.

There are places in this world where Christians are suffering just as Jesus did—unfair arrest, confinement, and trials as well as humiliation and false accusation, physical torture, and even death. Do you pray for them? How would you and I respond if we faced persecution at that level? Are we ashamed of Jesus? God forbid!

Statisticians tell us that more Christians were martyred in the twentieth century than in all the previous centuries combined. Peter warned the first-century churches that persecution was coming, and it came (1 Peter 4:12–19). God has judgment reserved for lost sinners, but "judgment will begin at the house of God" (v. 17). Are believers in the churches today prepared for this? Are you?

Judas committed suicide, but the other disciples ran for their lives, which is what Jesus told them to do (Zech. 13:7; Matt. 26:31–32). They met together with their risen Lord and He taught them personally until He ascended to glory (Acts 1:1–11). We may make a mess of things, but when the living Christ is at work, we are forgiven and given wisdom and power to do His will for His glory. The eminent Scottish preacher Alexander Whyte said, "The victorious Christian life is a series of new beginnings." Have you made a new beginning?

9

The Crucifixion of Jesus

Matthew 26–27; Mark 14–15; Luke 22–23; John 18–19

Every milestone that we visit with the Master ultimately leads us to Jerusalem and Calvary, because He was born to die for our sins. "Now My soul is troubled, and what shall I say? 'Father, save me from this hour?' But for this purpose I came to this hour" (John 12:27). At the very beginning of His ministry, His baptism pictured death, burial, and resurrection; and on the mount of Transfiguration, He and Moses and Elijah discussed His approaching crucifixion. As Jesus ministered from place to place, He knew that Golgotha was His destination. "He steadfastly set His face to go to Jerusalem" (Luke 9:51). Satan tempted Him with alternatives, Peter opposed His going to the cross (Matt. 16:21–28), and His followers could not understand the connection between suffering and glory (Luke 24:13–27). But if you take the cross out of the Scriptures, there is nothing left for sinners or for saints. Oswald Chambers wrote, "The central keystone for all Time and Eternity on which the whole purpose of God depends, is the cross."[1]

---

[1] Oswald Chambers, *Approved unto God* (Fort Washington, PA: Christian Literature Crusade, 1973), 39.

Years ago, Dr. A. W. Tozer warned us about a popular "new cross" that had eliminated sacrifice, separation from the world, and suffering for the sake of Jesus. "The old cross slew men; the new cross entertains them," he wrote in *The Divine Conquest*. "The old cross condemned; the new cross amuses. The old cross condemned confidence in the flesh; the new cross encourages it. The old cross brought tears and blood; the new cross brings laughter."[2]

As I entered a church one Lord's Day, a greeter smiled broadly as he gave me a service program and said, "Come in and have fun!" Unwittingly, he was promoting the new cross. When Jesus ascended to heaven, He took to the throne of the Father the Calvary wounds (not "scars") on His body. The people of God in heaven will be reminded forever that the way to glory was not cheap. No true believer had fun at Golgotha.

Perhaps the best way to deal with this subject is to answer five basic questions.

Who Was It Who Died?

The condemned party was Jesus Christ, the Son of God. He had committed no sins, He had broken no laws, He had caused no riots, He had injured nobody but had helped many. He went about doing good works (Acts 10:38) and proclaiming the good news of God's kingdom, and "the common people heard Him gladly" (Mark 12:37). But the religious leaders in Jerusalem opposed His ministry, rejected His message, and were envious of His success with the people (Matt. 27:18); so they engineered His arrest, conviction, and execution. As you read through the Gospel of John, you behold the faith of the disciples growing and the unbelief and hostility of the religious leaders increasing as well. The climax

---

[2]   A. W. Tozer, *The Divine Conquest* (Camp Hill, PA: Christian Publications, 1950), 59–60.

came at Calvary. When the leaders heard that Jesus was dead, they thought they had won a great victory, but actually they were the losers!

John wrote his Gospel to affirm and defend the fact that Jesus Christ is the Son of God and the Savior of the world (John 20:30–31). Very early in church history, false teachers had crept into the churches and were leading people astray (2 Peter 2), and their successors are still with us. John quotes a number of trustworthy witnesses who declared that Jesus is the Son of God come in the flesh. John the Baptist said, "And I have seen and testified that this is the Son of God" (John 1:34). Nathanael, one of the Lord's apostles, testified, "Rabbi, You are the Son of God" (John 1:49); and Peter, the leading disciple, said to Jesus, "Also we have come to believe and know that You are the Christ, the Son of the living God" (John 6:69). Martha, sister of Lazarus and Mary, called Him "the Christ, the Son of God" (John 11:27); and Jesus Himself affirmed that He was the Son of God (John 3:18; 5:25; 9:35; 10:36; 11:4). The Father even spoke from heaven and identified His beloved Son (Matt. 3:17; 17:5), and the demons knew who Jesus was and openly admitted it (Luke 4:41).

That Almighty God, the Creator of the universe, should humble Himself and come to earth to die for lost sinners is an amazing truth. To help us keep this remarkable truth alive in our hearts, Jesus instituted the Lord's Supper and instructed us to observe it in remembrance of Him (1 Cor. 11:23–26). The more you consider who Jesus is and how much He suffered to accomplish His work during those six hours He hung between heaven and earth, the more remarkable the divine plan of salvation becomes. I want to remember the *lives* of my loved ones and not their deaths, but I would have no spiritual life within me at all if Jesus had not died for me. Jesus died our death for us that we might share His life with Him and live for His glory. I don't know who first said that, but I hope I never forget it.

How Did Jesus Die?

The noun "cross" is found twenty-seven times in the New Testament and the verb "crucify" forty-six times in one form or another. Jesus was illegally arrested and tried, then humiliated and flogged, and finally led out and nailed to a Roman cross. Incited by the religious leaders, the Jewish mob had shouted to Pilate, "Away with Him! Crucify Him!" (John 19:15). They did not realize that this form of death had been decreed from eternity past. Moses (Deut. 21:22–23; see Gal. 3:13; Acts 5:30; 1 Peter 2:24) and David (Ps. 22:1–21) refer to crucifixion, and this is unusual because the Jews stoned people to death who were guilty of capital criminals. The Romans beheaded guilty criminals, but they had borrowed crucifixion from the Phoenicians. It was customary to announce the victim's crime on a placard nailed above his head, and the Roman governor Pontius Pilate wrote this one: "JESUS OF NAZARETH, THE KING OF THE JEWS." The Jewish religious leaders resented what he wrote and tried to persuade Pilate to change it, but the vacillating governor displayed unexpected courage and stood his ground (John 19:17–22). When the Lord God is not allowed to rule, He overrules and always accomplishes His purposes.

We could ponder the inhuman physical aspects of crucifixion but it would not be an edifying experience, for it was an ugly and excruciatingly painful form of death. The important thing is that Jesus was "obedient to the point of death, even the death of the cross" (Phil. 2:8), and accomplished the work the Father had given Him to do. He shouted, "It is finished," not "I am finished" (John 19:30). The tense of the verb means "it is finished, it stands finished, and it always will be finished." The important thing to remember is that Jesus did not die because the Roman soldiers murdered Him but because *He willingly gave His life for us.* "I lay down My life that I may take it again," said Jesus. "No one takes it from Me, but I lay it down of myself" (John 10:17–18). On three occasions, Jesus said He would be "lifted up," which is a direct reference to His crucifixion (John 3:14; 8:28; 12:32–34). Please relate those three references to what Jesus said in John 14:6.

Let me mention now (and we will discuss it later) that crucifixion is a form of death that you cannot perform on yourself. People can shoot themselves, poison themselves, drown themselves, cut their own throats, hang themselves, throw themselves down from a high place, gas themselves, starve themselves, throw themselves in front of a moving vehicle or into a machine, or smother themselves, but they cannot crucify themselves. Jesus willingly surrendered Himself to the Father and drank the cup that was prepared for Him to drink (John 18:10–11). This has tremendous significance to believers when it comes to gaining victory over the world, the flesh, and the devil.

When Did Jesus Die?

Jesus died at Passover, on the day when the Passover lambs were slain and the Jewish pilgrims in Jerusalem commemorated their nation's deliverance from Egypt. Under the old covenant, the lambs died for the people; but under the new covenant, the Shepherd would die for the sheep! Isaac asked his father Abraham, "Look, the fire and the wood, but where is the lamb for a burnt offering?" Abraham's reply stirs my heart: "My son, God will provide for Himself the lamb for a burnt offering" (Gen. 22:7–8). The immediate provision was a ram that took the place of Isaac on the altar (Gen. 22:13), but the ultimate answer was Jesus Christ, the Son of God, and there can be no replacement for Him.

The "lamb" sequence in Scripture is fascinating: "Where is the lamb?" asked young Isaac. "Behold! The Lamb of God," shouted John the Baptist (John 1:29). "Worthy is the Lamb that was slain!" shouted the saints and angels in heaven (Rev. 5:12). The original instructions for celebrating Passover are in Exodus 12 and they make it clear that faith in the Lamb must be personal. It reads "a lamb" (v. 3), "the lamb" (v. 4), and "your lamb" (v. 5). The lamb had to be without blemish (v. 5), and Peter informs us that Jesus qualified (1 Peter 1:18–19). Is Jesus Christ, the Son of God, *your* Lamb?

The Passover lamb was selected on the tenth day of the month and carefully examined and watched until the fourteenth day to make sure it had no defects, and then it was slain (Exod. 20:3, 6). The Jewish people and their religious leaders were given three years to watch Jesus and hear what He taught, *and they could find no fault in Him!* "Which of you convicts me of sin?" Jesus asked the crowd (John 8:46), and nobody accused Him. At the so-called trial, the leaders depended on false witnesses to condemn Jesus (Matt. 26:59–66). For three years they had rejected the true words of Jesus, the faithful witness (Rev. 1:5), and many people are making the same costly mistake today.

Why Did Jesus Die?

The gospel states it simply: "Christ died for our sins according to the Scriptures. . . . He was buried, and . . . He rose again the third day according to the Scriptures" (1 Cor. 15:3–4). John 3:16 is such a familiar verse that many Christians have lost the splendor of what it says, but it does tell the story clearly: God loves lost sinners, Christ died to save lost sinners, and that salvation is experienced when lost sinners trust Jesus Christ. Those who do not believe will perish; those who believe have eternal life. That is why Jesus died.

Jesus spent six hours on the cross; and from noon to three o'clock, darkness blanketed the whole land. At the end of that darkness He cried out, "My God, My God, why have you forsaken Me?" (Matt. 27:45–46). Was that darkness creation's way of grieving over the death of the Creator, or was it the Father's way of sheltering Jesus from the burning sun? Jesus said to the men who arrested Him in the garden, "But this is your hour, and the power of darkness" (Luke 22:53). More than one Bible student believes that the devil was at work in that darkness as the Father and the Son brought to completion the great plan of salvation. When on the cross Jesus was made sin for you and me (2 Cor. 5:21; 1 Peter 2:24), for a moment the Father turned His face away from His Son (Hab. 2:13)—and Jesus won the victory over Satan, sin, and death! "He has delivered us from the power of darkness and has translated us into the kingdom of the Son of His love" (Col. 1:13).

Luke 23:45 informs us that, at that same time, "the veil of the temple was torn in two." This veil hung between the holy place and the holy of holies where the ark of the covenant rested, and the high priest was the only person allowed to enter that chamber, and then only once a year on the Day of Atonement (Heb. 7). But now the veil was torn, and the child of God could go into the very presence of God to worship and to pray! Jesus has gone before us into the heavenly sanctuary and the way into the holiest is available (Heb. 6:18–20; 10:20–25). The old covenant was set aside and the new covenant was ushered in.

The priesthood made nothing perfect (Heb. 7:11), but now in Christ we have a perfect high priest who intercedes for us in heaven. The old covenant sacrifices made nothing perfect (Heb. 10:1–3), but Jesus "by one offering . . . has perfected forever those who are being sanctified" (Heb. 10:14). The law made nothing perfect (Heb. 7:19), but the grace of God ministered by the Holy Spirit moves us toward perfection and spiritual maturity (Heb. 13:20–21). The old covenant law was nailed to the cross (Col. 2:14) and we are no longer in bondage to its demands (Rom. 6:14). It is because of the cross that we have peace with

God (Col. 1:20) and are reconciled to God (Eph. 4:16). Because of the cross Satan and his hosts have been defeated (Col. 2:13–15) and we can live in victory over the old nature within us and the world system around us (Gal. 5:24; 6:14).

For Whom Did Jesus Die?

John the Baptist announced that Jesus was the Lamb of God that "takes away the sin of the world" (John 1:29). The blood of the sanctuary sacrifices only *covered* sin (Pss. 32:1; 85:2; Heb. 10:4), and the forgiveness God granted the worshiper was based on the future sacrifice of Jesus on the cross. But since that great victory on the cross, "whoever calls on the name of the Lord shall be saved" (Acts 2:21). Paul affirms that "one died for all" (2 Cor. 5:14) and that the Lord "desires all men to be saved" (1 Tim. 2:4). Jesus is "the Savior of all men, especially of those who believe" (1 Tim. 4:10). Jesus "tasted death for everyone" (Heb. 2:9) but, like the people in Jerusalem over whom Jesus wept, many people "will not believe" (Matt. 23:37).

The apostle John writes that "the Father has sent the Son as Savior of the world" (1 John 4:14), but it's obvious that the whole world will not trust Jesus Christ. Jesus will separate the sheep from the goats (Matt. 25:31–46) and the wheat from the weeds (Matt 13:36–45). It is His elect people who hear the gospel, admit their sins, believe on Jesus, and are born into God's family. Why did Paul in his ministry endure shipwreck, imprisonments, hunger, beatings, and other trials? Because he knew that God had His elect people! "Therefore I endure all things for the sake of the elect, that they also may obtain the salvation which is in Christ Jesus with eternal glory" (2 Tim. 2:10). Paul did not know who God's elect were until they were saved, but he knew that his praying and his preaching of the cross would produce a harvest. Jesus said, "My sheep hear My voice, and I know them, and they follow

Me. And I give them eternal life, and they shall never perish, neither shall anyone snatch them out of My hand" (John 10:27–28).

A well-known preacher said that preaching over the radio was like an eye doctor standing at the top of the Empire State Building in New York City, trying to get a drop of medicine into the eye of a patient on the sidewalk below. It's not a bad analogy except for one thing: God controls the rain and can put each drop exactly where He wants it (Isa. 55:10–11), and He can do the same with His word. In my years of ministry I have made many radio programs and entrusted them to the Lord to accomplish His will. When you sit in a studio and tape a program that will be broadcast perhaps two months later, you have to depend on the guidance of the Lord.

The late Theodore Epp, founder and speaker for Back to the Bible Broadcast, was taping a message one day and felt led to say, "You there—lady with the clothes basket—put it down and listen to me." When the message was broadcast weeks later, there was a woman coming up from the basement in her house and carrying a basket of clothes! She heard Mr. Epp's words as she entered the kitchen, put down the basket, and sat down to listen—and she believed and was born again! God knows His elect. Our job is to be faithful to sow the seed, pray, and trust God to do the rest.

God does not have to save anybody! Whoever is saved is saved by grace. From the human viewpoint, the Lord has three choices. He can save everybody, but then where is His justice? He can save nobody, but then where is His love? He can save an elect group by grace and glorify Himself in them. That is obviously His choice. "'The Lord knows those that are His,' and, 'Let everyone who names the name of Christ depart from iniquity'" (2 Tim. 2:19). The proof that we are among the elect is that we live like Christ and for Christ. That's how the lost world can tell we are Christians.

According to Ephesians 1:3–14, each Person in the Godhead is involved in our salvation. We are chosen by the Father (vv. 3–6), purchased by the Son (7–12), and sealed by the Spirit (vv. 13–14), and it is all to the praise and glory of the Lord (vv. 6, 12, and 14). As far as the Father is concerned, I was saved when He chose me in Christ before the foundation of the world, but I knew nothing about that until after I was saved. As far as the Savior is concerned, I was saved when He died for me on the cross, and I heard that in the gospel message. As far as the Holy Spirit is concerned, I was saved when He convicted me of my unbelief and I trusted Christ and was born again. Everything came together that the Trinity had planned. Then I could say with Paul that He "loved me and gave Himself for me" (Gal. 2:20). Unless salvation is personal, it is not salvation at all.

The apostle Peter agrees with Paul's Trinitarian view of redemption: "elect according to the foreknowledge of God the Father, in sanctification of the Spirit, for obedience and sprinkling of the blood of Jesus Christ" (1 Peter 1:2). The word "foreknowledge" does not mean simply that God knew beforehand who would believe, but that God *chose them beforehand to believe and be saved*. Dr. H. A. Ironside said, "Salvation is like a sinner seeing a door with a sign over it that reads 'WHOSOEVER WILL MAY COME.' The sinner goes through the door and turns around and sees another sign which reads 'CHOSEN IN CHRIST BEFORE THE FOUNDATION OF THE WORLD' (Eph. 1:4)." Why should the Lord choose us? Who are we or what have we done that we should become God's children? He chose us because He loves us and the whole transaction is a matter of divine grace and not human merit (Eph. 2:8–9). We are saved by grace and kept by grace; we live by grace and serve by grace. We say with Paul, "But by the grace of God I am what I am" (1 Cor. 15:10).

What Should the Cross Mean to Believers Today?

Our personal attitude toward the cross of Christ indicates our spiritual condition. Lost people may have sentimental feelings about the death of Jesus, especially during Lent, but it makes no lasting spiritual difference in their everyday lives. It has well been said that sentiment is feeling without responsibility. True believers have come to the cross by faith, trusted Jesus for salvation, and taken up the cross to follow Him. This means identifying openly with Jesus and carrying the cross for His glory (Matt. 10:34–39). We have been reconciled to God by the cross (Eph. 2:1 6) and received peace (Col. 1:20); we have died with Christ and been raised to new life. Accept this by faith!

Since this is true, we have a new relationship to our three enemies—the world, the flesh, and the devil (Eph. 2:1–3). Christ died for us *and we died with Him!* "I have been crucified with Christ; it is no longer I who live, but Christ lives in me; and the life which I now live in the flesh I live by faith in the Son of God, who loved me and gave Himself for me" (Gal. 2:20). Jesus took our place on the cross and our faith in that *substitution* saves us; but we have also died with Him on that cross, and that *identification* enables us to live a victorious life. In Christ we have died to the world (Gal. 6:14), to the old sinful nature (Gal. 5:24), and to our enemy the devil (John 12:31; Col. 1:13).

The hymn "When I Survey the Wondrous Cross" by Isaac Watts has long been a favorite of mine. The original title was "Crucifixion to the World, by the Cross of Christ" because the hymn is based on Galatians 6:14: "But God forbid that I should glory except in the cross of our Lord Jesus Christ, by whom the world has been crucified to me, and I to the world." Over the years the name of the hymn has been changed and the people who edit hymnals have eliminated the fourth verse.

> His dying crimson, like a robe,
> > Spreads o'er His body on the tree;
> Then I am dead to all the globe,
> > And all the globe is dead to me.

I admit that verse four is not the greatest piece of poetry Isaac Watts ever wrote, *but its message is desperately needed by the church today!* Jesus gave His life to take us out of the world so He could set us apart and send us back into the world to be godly witnesses (John 17:14–18). One day we shall leave this world and go to heaven. How sad when people in church leadership become influenced by the methods of the world and the wisdom of the world, and start to lead others into imitating the ways of the world (Rom. 12:2). What we need are churches with ministries that are biblical and members who are not ashamed of the gospel of Christ. The world has crept into the church, and when the world comes in, the cross goes out. I recall when the liberal theologians laughed and called the message of the cross "butcher shop religion." I don't hear that today, but neither do I always find the message of the cross in the sermons and songs.

Christians are supposed to glory in the cross (Gal. 6:14), and we can glory in the cross *because the cross is in glory today!* When Jesus returned to heaven, He took the wounds of the cross with Him in His glorified feet and hands and side. If the saints in heaven glory in the cross, why are the saints on earth silent? The Lamb of God in heaven bears the marks of being *slain* (Rev. 5:6, 9, 12; 13:8) and is honored because of it. The Christians who ignore or minimize the cross today will have to do some adjusting when they get to heaven. What do these people really think when they gather for the Lord's Supper?

We have experienced a miracle because of the cross, and because of the cross we have a message to share with the lost world.

"But we preach Christ crucified" (1 Cor. 1:23). "For I determined not to know anything among you except Jesus Christ and Him crucified" (1 Cor. 2:2). Our witness focuses on Christ and the cross, what He has done to rescue lost sinners. No matter what text the minister preaches and no matter what lesson the teacher teaches, they must end at the cross and a loving appeal to sinners to be saved. Many religious people are like that Ethiopian officer that Philip met on the desert road (Acts 8:26–40). They read about the cross or hear about it but don't understand what it means. Philip explained the cross of Christ to the Ethiopian and he believed in Christ and was saved. That is the kind of witnessing we need today.

The cross reminds us that our heavenly Father loves us. Many old covenant Jews thought that health, wealth, and a large, beautiful family were the evidences of God's love, but many unbelievers have those blessings and never give God thanks. "But God demonstrates His own love toward us that while we were still sinners, Christ died for us" (Rom. 5:8). The next time you are discouraged and Satan is telling you that God doesn't care, remember Calvary and give thanks that Jesus died for you. When you have done your best yet you are criticized, remember the cross and realize it is worth it all. When you are flat on your back and the people who ought to help you are ignoring you, remember Calvary. Our Lord's suffering and death announce to you and me that what looks like defeat in the Christian life turns out to be victory. Be patient and see what the Lord will do. The cross speaks of the blood of Christ and the blood of Christ speaks of forgiveness (Matt. 26:28), a right standing before God (Rom. 5:7), cleansing (Heb. 9:14; 1 John 1:7), redemption (1 Peter 1:18–19), and victory (Rev. 1:5; 12:11).

If we are faithfully carrying the cross Jesus has given us, we will have no problem bearing witness to the crucified Christ. Jesus gave His all for us and the Spirit enables us to give our all to Him. It's possible for us to be so careless in our Christian walk that we actually rob the cross of power (1 Cor. 1:17). "For though He was crucified in weakness, He lives by the power of God" (2 Cor. 13:4). "But you shall receive power when the Holy Spirit has come upon you, and you shall be witnesses to Me" (Acts 1:8).

We often discuss what the cross did to Jesus, but have you ever considered what Jesus did to the cross? In the Roman Empire, the cross meant defeat, but Jesus turned it into victory. Paul closes the great "death and resurrection" chapter of 1 Corinthians 15 with, "But thanks be to God, who gives us the victory through our Lord Jesus Christ," followed by the "steadfast" benediction. To the Romans, the cross meant suffering and shame, but Jesus transformed it into glory to God so that we "glory in the cross" for Jesus' sake (Gal. 6:14). Crucifixion was the worst possible death, but because of the cross we have everlasting life (Gal. 2:20). In the ancient world, the cross was so terrible that it was not mentioned in decent conversation, but today people spend money to purchase little crosses to wear on their person to let people know they are followers of Jesus Christ. In our witnessing we may speak about the cross without apology.

(*The Milestone Mirror: A Pause for Reflection*)

William Penn, founder of the Quakers, used to say, "No cross, no crown!" What does that mean to you? If we are "crucified with Christ" (Gal. 2:20), how will that change our lives?

We see crosses on gravestones in cemeteries as well as on church buildings, and we see people wearing crosses as jewelry. But according to Jesus, what more is involved? The cross speaks of submission, shame, suffering, and service to others. Do we live that way, carrying our crosses?

Joseph of Arimathea and Nicodemus removed our Lord's body from the cross and buried it in Joseph's new tomb (John 19:38–42). According to Jewish law, touching a dead body defiled them, which meant they could not observe Passover. If you were to ask them if they cared, what do you think their answers would be?

When God's people get to heaven, they will have glorified bodies as does Jesus today, except that He has the marks of the cross on His glorified body. Why?

10

The Resurrection of Jesus

Matthew 28; Mark 16; Luke 24; John 20–21;
1 Corinthians 15

The resurrection of Jesus Christ from the dead was an event that changed everything in that first fellowship of believers and it can change everything in our lives and churches today. Whenever a sinner turns to the Lord for salvation, the resurrected Christ forgives sin and imparts eternal life (Rom. 10:9–13). Whenever a troubled believer cries out for help, the living Christ hears and answers from the throne of grace (Heb. 4:14–16). When believers gather to worship, they address their praise and prayers to the living Lord and experience His blessing (Acts 4:23–31; 16:25–34). If the church is dead, it's because the people have forgotten that Jesus is alive.

Dr. R. W. Dale (1829–1895) was a leading British pastor and theologian who ministered at the Carr's Lane Congregational Church, Birmingham, from 1854 until his death. One day while preparing an Easter Sunday message, he was so struck by the reality of the Lord's resurrection that he began to walk about his study saying out loud, "Christ is alive! He is alive! He lives— He lives!" From that time on, he always selected a resurrection hymn for each Sunday morning worship service. How it would change our congregations today if we really grasped the significance of our Lord's resurrection and allowed "the power of His resurrection" to grip us (Phil. 3:10).

Let's consider some important facts about our Lord's resurrection and see what they mean to us today.

Jesus Was Buried with Dignity

When criminals died at Golgotha, their bodies were usually treated like garbage and thrown into the smoldering refuse in the valley of the son of Hinnom, better known as Gehenna. To the Jews, an unburied corpse meant public disgrace and judgment from God. Furthermore, Psalm 16:8–11 predicted that Messiah's body would not see corruption. Peter quoted that promise in his message at Pentecost (Acts 2:22–28). But the Father had hidden two disciples in the Sanhedrin, Jews of high repute and influence, and they worked together to make sure Jesus had a decent burial.

We must remember that our Lord's burial is a part of the gospel message as recorded in 1 Corinthians 15:1–11. The phrase in v. 4 "and that He was buried" is brief but important; for the fact that Jesus was buried is proof that He actually died. The Roman soldiers knew their job and did it well. If the victims were lingering, the soldiers broke their legs or pierced their side and hastened their demise. The soldiers made sure Jesus was dead before they obeyed Pilate's order to give His body to Joseph of Arimathea (John 20:38–42). Joseph and Nicodemus wrapped the body in strips of linen along with the spices they brought and reverently placed our Lord's body in the tomb. Joseph rolled a great stone across the entrance which an angel would later roll back.

We meet Nicodemus three times in the Gospel of John: when he visited Jesus at night and learned about the new birth (John 3), when he defended Jesus in the Sanhedrin meeting (John 7:45–52), and when he and Joseph interred the body. Nicodemus had visited Jesus at night probably so there would be no interference, but when he helped Joseph bury Jesus, it was in broad daylight when others could see them. I have long believed that Nicodemus and Joseph of Arimathea had been meeting together to study the Scriptures and had concluded that Jesus was indeed the Messiah. By handling a dead body, they were ceremonially defiled and could not eat the Passover, but it made no difference because they had found and trusted "the Lamb of God who takes away the sin of the world" (John 1:29).

Nicodemus and Joseph had learned from the Scriptures that the Messiah would be rejected and crucified at Passover, and God led them to protect the body. Why would a wealthy and influential man like Joseph have a family tomb in the shadow of Golgotha where noisy crowds gathered to watch criminals be crucified? Would you want your burial place adjacent to the stockyards? *Joseph did not prepare the tomb for himself but for Jesus!* He and Nicodemus were in the tomb with the spices during those six hours Jesus was on the cross. When they heard Jesus cry, "It is finished," Nicodemus kept guard and Joseph went to see Pilate and got permission to inter the body. There are those who deny the resurrection by claiming that Jesus did not die but only swooned and then revived in the tomb, but the Roman soldiers and two members of the Sanhedrin can bear witness that Jesus actually died. So can the prophet Isaiah (53:8–12). The Roman soldiers expected to dispose of the body of Jesus with the bodies of the two wicked thieves, but the Father had other plans. "And they made His grave with the wicked—but with the rich in His death" (Isa. 53:9). Because they were faithful, Joseph and Nicodemus helped to keep the message of the gospel pure: "Christ died for our sins according to the Scriptures, and . . . He was buried"— buried in dignity with the rich!

Jesus Was Raised in Victory

Early in His ministry, when Jesus was challenged for cleansing the temple, His reply was, "Destroy this temple, and in three days I will raise it up" (John 2:19). This was our Lord's first announcement of His death and resurrection as far as the gospel records are concerned. Later, when Peter declared his faith in Jesus Christ as the Son of God, Jesus began to teach the apostles that He would be crucified and buried and then be raised from the dead on the third day (Matt. 16:13–23). He repeated this truth after His transfiguration (Matt. 17:22–23) and as He made His way to Jerusalem with His disciples (Matt. 20:17–19). Had His followers taken this word to heart, they would not have been so confused and depressed when Jesus was crucified and laid in the tomb. Strangely enough, our Lord's enemies remembered His words! They asked Pilate to seal the tomb and post guards lest somebody fabricate a "resurrection" by stealing the body of Jesus (Matt. 27:62–66). But these religious leaders were defying the holy Trinity, for the Father raised Jesus from the dead (Acts 2:22; 3:15; 4:10), the Son raised Himself (John 2:19; 10:17–18), and the Spirit raised the Son (Rom. 1:4; 1 Peter 1:11; 3:18).

Our Lord's crucifixion looked like utter defeat, but the resurrection declared Calvary to be the greatest victory ever achieved on earth. He went from weakness to power, from humiliation to glory (Phil. 2:5–11), from the limitations of humanity to the freedom of deity, from a tomb to a throne. He won a decisive victory over the world (John 16:31; Gal. 6:14), the flesh (Rom. 6:5), and the devil (John 12:31–32; Col. 2:15). In fact, the death of the Savior brought about the death of death itself! "Our Savior Jesus Christ . . . has abolished death and brought life and immortality to light through the gospel" (2 Tim. 1:10). The word translated "abolished" means "to break the power and render inoperative." According to Romans 5, death still reigns (vv. 14, 17) because sin reigns (v. 21); but through Jesus Christ, grace reigns (vv. 17, 21) – *and God's people can "reign in life" through Jesus Christ* (v. 17)! We possess eternal life because we trust Jesus who is the resurrection and the life (John 11:25–26); and we can shout with Paul, "But thanks be to God, who gives us the victory through our Lord Jesus Christ" (1 Cor. 15:57). When a loved one dies, we who remain sorrow but "not as others who have no hope" (1 Thess. 4:13).

According to 1 Corinthians 15, because Jesus has disarmed and defeated death, we have something to believe in (vv. 16–17), something to talk about (vv. 14–15), something to take comfort from (v. 18), and something to look forward to (v. 19). Peter clearly declared this victory in his Pentecost sermon: "Jesus of Nazareth . . . whom God raised up, having loosed the pains of death, because it was not possible that He should be held by it" (Acts 2:22, 24). The empty tomb testified that Jesus had passed through the cocoon-like wrappings and left them intact. John and Peter saw the empty grave clothes and were convinced Jesus was alive (John 20:1–10).

When Paul uses the phrase "according to the Scriptures" in 1 Corinthians 15:3–4, he is referring, of course, to the Old Testament Scriptures that spoke in prophecy and type of the death and resurrection of Jesus Christ. Jesus Himself referred to Jonah, who spent three days and three nights in the great fish before being released (Matt. 12:38–41). The feast of firstfruits, celebrated on the third day after Passover (Lev. 23:9–12), pictures the resurrection of "Christ the firstfruits" (1 Cor. 15:20–23). Psalm 16:8–11 is quoted in Acts 2:23–28; Psalm 2:7 in Acts 13:33; Psalm 110:1 in Acts 2:34–35; and Psalm 34:20 in John 19:36. (See also Isaiah 53:10, Zechariah 12:10, and Psalm 118:15–24.) The Old Testament writers bear witness of our Lord's suffering, death, and resurrection.

Jesus Was Active in Ministry

After His resurrection, our Lord did not indulge in a "time of recuperation" from His sufferings and death but from the beginning was actively ministering to His grief-stricken followers, appearing to them and assuring them that He was alive. (See 1 Cor. 15:1–11.) The apostles were commissioned to be "witnesses of the resurrection" (Acts 1:22). Many of the people in Jerusalem knew that Jesus of Nazareth had been crucified; now they needed to know that He was alive and able to save all who would believe.

Mary Magdalene discovered the open tomb and jumped to the erroneous conclusion that somebody had stolen the body. She ran to tell Peter, and Peter and John ran to the tomb. The stone had been rolled back, so they went in and saw the empty grave-clothes. They were convinced that Jesus was alive (John 20:1–10). But it's one thing to see evidence and quite something else to meet the living Christ Himself! Mary lingered at the tomb and met Jesus but thought He was the gardener. When Jesus spoke her name, she recognized Him, and He turned her confusion into certainty. We may know all the theological arguments for the resurrection of Jesus, but it is the presence of the living Christ in our own daily experience that enables us to live for Him and serve Him.

When it came to meeting the disciples, Jesus turned their fears and doubts into faith and devotion (John 20:19–23). Jesus can walk through locked doors! Jesus had already spoken to Peter privately and restored him to fellowship (Mark 16:7; 1 Cor. 15:5), but He needed to restore him publicly to discipleship, for He had called him publicly (Luke 5:1–11); and John 21 describes how Jesus did it. Peter had gone fishing with six other disciples and they fished all night and caught nothing. Jesus appeared on the shore but they didn't recognize Him, and when they obeyed His orders, they caught 153 fish! Instantly, Peter knew it was the Master. The resurrected Christ can transform failure into success.

Perhaps the most dramatic appearance Jesus made after His resurrection and ascension was to Saul of Tarsus when he was on his way to persecute the saints in Damascus (Acts 9). Saul thought Jesus was dead, that his disciples had stolen the body from the tomb and hidden it (Matt. 28:11–15); but now he learned that Jesus was alive! When Saul trusted the living Christ, he was transformed from a persecutor into a preacher! He became Paul, the servant of Jesus Christ.

The living Christ is still active in ministry. He promised, "I am with you always, even to the end of the age" (Matt. 28:20). He warns us that "without Me, you can do nothing" (John 15:5). Woe to those children of God who think they can bear fruit without abiding in Jesus the true vine! The Holy Spirit is "the Spirit of life in Christ Jesus" (Rom. 8:2); and if we are filled with the Spirit and walking in the Spirit, we will be faithful and fruitful to the glory of God.

We look upon the first day of the week as the Lord's Day, and it is. The early church met and worshiped on resurrection day, the first day of the week. But we must realize that *every day is the Lord's Day if Jesus is our Lord!* We need not fear life or death, past sins or future challenges, physical burdens or spiritual battles or any enemy. We are more than conquerors through Him who loves us and lives for us and lives in us by His Spirit (Rom. 8:37–39)! Death has no sting because it ushers us into glory, and the grave has no victory because it will be emptied when Jesus comes (1 Cor. 15:50–58)! When we visit the graves of Christian loved ones, we must remember that Paul compared the burial of a body to the planting of a seed (1 Cor. 15:35–49). It may seem like winter as we sorrow, but "spring" will come when Jesus returns and the "seeds" planted will burst forth in power and beauty. Hallelujah!

Jesus Is Serious about Responsibility

Two instructions from an Easter angel clearly announce our responsibilities as God's people: "Come and see" the empty tomb and "Go and tell" the needy world (Matt. 28:6–7).

My wife and I have visited Jerusalem and seen what scholars tell us is the empty tomb of Jesus. But my assurance of a living Savior and Lord comes not from that visit but from the testimony of ancient witnesses whose words are recorded in the inspired Scriptures. The entire Bible testifies that Jesus is alive and ministering to us today from heaven, but more about that in the following chapter.

The way the apostle Peter uses the word "living" in his first epistle suggests that he was really gripped by the reality of his Master's resurrection. He states that Jesus is alive and is the "living stone" (1 Peter 2:4). Therefore God's children have a "living hope" (1 Peter 1:3), possess the living word of God (1:23), and are themselves "living stones" in the temple of God (2:5), the church that the Lord is building "for a habitation of God in the Spirit" (Eph. 2:21). In the midst of an evil world that is "dead in trespasses and sins" (Eph. 2:1), true Christians are alive in Christ and have the privilege and responsibility to "go and tell." We bear witness to the reality of the resurrection by the lives that we live and the words that we speak. It's sad that some churches manifest no life at all in their gatherings, but simply carry on business as usual; but we rejoice at those congregations that manifest His life and love not just on Sundays but all week long.

"Come and see! Go and tell!" These are six simple words that every believer can easily understand. And now that we understand them, let's obey them.

(*The Milestone Mirror: A Pause for Reflection*)

The Master had told His followers several times
that He would be raised from the dead the third
day after His crucifixion, but somehow His
words did not sink in. Like the birds that pick up
the seeds on the ground, Satan snatches away the
"Scripture seeds" Jesus plants in hearts not prepared to receive the word of God (Matt. 13:1–9,
18–23). Do you prepare your heart for God's
truth by confessing sin and humbling yourself
before the Lord? Do you think about it during
the day and ask the Spirit to teach you?

Jesus is alive today and we may fully trust Him
to care for us. Do you think of Him, talk to Him,
and obey Him during the day and thank Him for
His presence with you? Like Nehemiah, do you
send quick "e-mail prayers" up to heaven during
the day?

The word "empty" is important in the Christian life. The manger is empty even though we
celebrate our Lord's birth annually. The cross is
empty because His death completed the work of
redemption. The tomb and grave clothes were
empty because Jesus is alive and ministering as
our High Priest in heaven. Because of the work
of Christ, *we can experience fullness!* Ponder John
1:16, Ephesians 3:19 and 4:13, and Colossians 1:19
and 2:9.

11

The Ascension of Jesus to Heaven

Mark 16:19–20; Luke 24:44–52; Acts 1:1–12;
Ephesians 1:15–23; Philippians 2:9–11

Jesus began His earthly ministry by being tempted forty days by the devil (Matt. 4:2), and He closed His earthly ministry by spending forty days with His followers "speaking of the things pertaining to the kingdom of God" (Acts 1:1–3). Unfortunately His disciples were more interested in restoring the kingdom of Israel, but Jesus was focusing on present ministry and not on the past. He promised to send the Holy Spirit to enable them to bear witness of Him and declare the gospel, and He climaxed His last meeting with them by ascending to heaven (Acts 1:4–11). For centuries, Christians have celebrated Ascension Day forty days after Easter, reminding themselves of the living Christ ministering in heaven and the enabling Holy Spirit giving power to the church on earth. God's people today desperately need to learn what the glorified Son of God is doing for them in heaven today and to draw upon the Holy Spirit's power.

Jesus Went Up to Heaven and Sat Down

Our Lord had told His disciples He would return to the Father, so seeing Jesus go up into the clouds should not have surprised them

(Luke 24:26; John 7:33–34; 13:3; 14:1–4, 28; 16:5, 7, 10, 16–19, 28). His work on earth was finished and His followers were prepared to serve Him. It was now time to begin His unfinished work in heaven so His people on earth could continue the work of winning the lost. Philippians 2:1–11 describes His "descent" and "ascent," emptying Himself and becoming a servant and then ascending to heaven to fill all things (Eph. 4:9–10). Dr. James S. Stewart says it best: "For it was not to desert history that Christ returned to the Father, but to bind history to Himself forever."[1] Jesus in heaven is ministering on earth by His Spirit working in and through His people.

You would not find chairs in the Jewish tabernacle or in the temple, because the priests' work was never finished. "For it is not possible that the blood of bulls and goats could take away sins," but "this Man, after He had offered one sacrifice for sins forever, sat down at the right hand of God" (Heb. 10:4, 12). "The Lord said to my Lord, 'Sit at My right hand, till I make Your enemies Your footstool'" (Ps. 110:1). This "coronation" psalm is quoted twenty-one times in the Bible, including five times in the book of Hebrews. Jesus was "received up in glory" (1 Tim. 3:16) and is enthroned in heaven "far above all principality and power and might and dominion, and every name that is named, not only in this age, but also in that which is to come" (Eph. 1:21; Acts 2:34–36; 1 Peter 3:22). Hallelujah!

It is important to remember that the moment you trusted Christ as Savior and Lord, the Holy Spirit entered your body and made it His temple. His presence has identified you with Jesus Christ in His death, burial, and resurrection (Rom. 6:1–7; Gal. 2:20) as well as in His ascension and enthronement (Eph. 2:1–10). We are seated with Him in the heavenly places and by faith we can draw upon His spiritual power and riches. The

---

[1] James S. Stewart, *Thine Is the Kingdom* (Edinburgh: St. Andrew Press, 1956), 72.

phrases "in Christ," "in Him," and "in the Lord" are used 164 times in Paul's writings to describe our living union with our living Lord. We are seated on the throne with Him, the angels minister on our behalf (Heb. 2:14), and believing prayer gives us access to the throne of grace (Heb. 4:16).

Our Master's ministry in heaven is that of high priest (Heb. 4:14), advocate (1 John 2:1), forerunner (Heb. 6:20), and mediator/intercessor (1 Tim. 2:5; Heb. 7:25). As high priest, Jesus gives us the grace we need to know God's will and do it and to overcome temptation and live victoriously (Heb. 4:14–16). If we do sin, He is our advocate so that we may confess our sins and be forgiven (1 John 1:5–2:2). The victorious Christian life is a series of new beginnings that draw us closer to God. As forerunner (Heb. 6:20), Jesus has gone before us into the heavenly sanctuary so that we may follow Him, fellowship with Him, and receive the grace we need. We are saved by His death from the penalty of sin, but we are being saved by His life from the power and pollution of sin (Rom. 5:10). Paul calls this "reigning in life" (Rom. 5:17).

"If then you were raised with Christ, seek those things which are above, where Christ is, sitting at the right hand of God. Set your mind on things above, not on things on the earth" (Col. 3:1–2). Our Lord is mediator and intercessor between us and the Father. "For there is one God and one Mediator between God and men, the Man Christ Jesus" (1 Tim. 2:5). The Son has intercessory ministry in heaven and the Spirit has intercessory ministry within the temple of our body (Rom. 8:26–27). We may experience the love of God—Father and Son and Holy Spirit—and we may share our love with them (John 14:23–24).

Jesus in Heaven Gives and Receives

When He died on the cross, Jesus gave His all to save a sinful world. Now glorified in heaven, He gives His all to His church, the people who have trusted Him and are serving Him. Jesus in heaven is not interceding for the lost world (John 17:9) but for His own people here on earth. Jesus wants to receive from His church prayer, praise, and obedient service, and He wants to give to the church spiritual gifts, an understanding of His word, power for witnessing, working, and walking in His will, and "grace to help in time of need" (Heb. 4:16). Only He can supply what we need, and He is willing to do it (Phil. 4:19).

The most important part of my day is in the morning when I get alone with the Lord, read His Word and meditate on it, and then fellowship with Him in worship and prayer, waiting before Him for the strength and guidance I need for that day. God has "in these last days spoken to us by His Son" (Heb. 1:1–2), and I am grateful for the way the Holy Spirit teaches us from the Scriptures. There are times when the Lord awakens me at night and shares a spiritual truth with me, just what I have needed for my own life or for a sermon or a chapter of a book. I keep a small lamp and a pad of paper on my bedside table so I can write down immediately what the Lord is teaching me; otherwise, I may go back to sleep and forget what the Lord taught me.

Our giving to God doesn't "purchase" the blessings we receive, because everything the Lord provides is a gift of His grace. "And my God shall supply all your need according to His riches in glory by Christ Jesus" (Phil. 4:19). One of the purposes for Christ's enthronement in glory is that He might distribute His gifts to believers around the world (Ps. 68:18; Eph. 4:7–12). The Holy Spirit equips each believer with the gift or gifts needed to do the work God has called her or him to do (Eph. 4:12–16). It's tragic when people without the required spiritual gifts are placed in church offices, because they simply cannot do the job the way God wants it done and they become stumbling blocks instead of stepping stones. It takes more than a pleasing personality and a willingness to work for a person to serve the Lord. We also need the gifting that only the Holy Spirit can provide.

What are the gifts the Master would be pleased to receive from us—and remember that anything we give Him has first been given to us by the Lord. David made that very clear: "For all things come from You, and of Your own we have given You" (1 Chron. 29:14). He wants my heart and my love (Prov. 23:26) as well as my body, mind, and will (Rom. 12:1–2). I should be generous in giving of whatever wealth He provides (Mal. 3:10; Acts 20:35; 2 Cor. 9:6–11). He deserves my time, not only for prayer and Bible study, but also for serving others (Eph. 5:15–17); and certainly I should give Him my best on the Lord's Day. Have you read lately our Lord's promise in Luke 6:38?

What does our generous Lord give to us? He gives us salvation (Eph. 2:8–9), all the grace that we need (James 4:6), our daily bread (Matt. 6:11), the precious word of God (John 17:8), the Holy Spirit (John 14:16), strength for the journey (Isa. 40:29–31)—and all the things we need for life and service (Rom. 8:32). He gave the people of Israel a special land and He will give His saints a home in heaven (John 14:1–6). I could go on, but if you have been walking with the Lord any length of time, you know from experience that we cannot out-give God.

Jesus Goes Before Us and Stands Against Our Enemies

"And when he brings out his own sheep, he goes before them; and the sheep follow him, for they know his voice" (John 10:4). Our Lord's voice is heard in the Scriptures; when you open your Bible, God opens His mouth. Unbelievers have no special love for or attraction to the word of God, but to dedicated believers, knowing the Bible is absolutely essential for it is the voice of the shepherd.

You can drive cattle, but you cannot drive sheep. They must be led. The sheep recognize the voice of the shepherd but will not respond to the voice of a stranger (John 10:1–4). During many years of itinerant ministry, my wife and I have been grateful for the leading of the Lord. He has helped us in our planning and guided us in our traveling, and when things appeared to be confusing, He has always led us through to our destination. In my daily devotions, I pray "The Lord's Prayer" (Matt. 6:9–12) because it covers so many aspects of life, including the will of God and deliverance from evil and the evil one.

Jesus goes before us to prepare the way, and He stands with us against enemies that want to oppose us. We will not know until we get to heaven how many times we have been protected from danger as we have gone about our daily lives and our assigned ministries. As the people of Israel prepared to enter the Promised Land, Moses said to them, "Do not be terrified, or be afraid of them. The Lord your God, who goes before you, He will fight for you" (Deut. 1:29–30). The prophet Isaiah wrote, "For you shall not go out in haste, nor go by flight, for the Lord will go before you, and the God of Israel will be your rear guard" (52:12).

I once heard a preacher use the word "lucky" in his message as he spoke about the leading of the Lord in his life, and I was startled. The word "luck" is not in the Christian vocabulary; we prefer to speak about "the providence of God" or "the leading of the Lord." Abraham's servant said, "As for me, being on the way, the Lord led me" (Gen. 24:27). If we are willing to obey the Lord and wait upon Him, He will show us the way we ought to take. "If anyone *wants* to do His will, he shall know concerning the doctrine," said Jesus (John 7:17; italics mine). God's will is not a buffet that offers us a variety of choices, nor do we dare make a choice and say within our heart, "If I don't like it, I can always do something else." When we ask God to show us His will, we must in our heart say, "And I will obey it."

When the angry mob stoned Stephen, Jesus stood up in heaven and revealed Himself to His faithful servant, as if He were saying, "I'm standing with you" (Acts 7:54–60)! When Paul was opposed in Corinth, the Lord stood with him, and Paul stayed in the city for eighteen months serving the Lord (Acts 18:9–11). At the close of Paul's ministry, he wrote to Timothy, "At my first defense no one stood with me, but all forsook me. May it not be charged against them. But the Lord stood with me and strengthened me . . . [and] I was delivered out of the mouth of the lion" (2 Tim. 4:16–17). Jesus goes before us to prepare the way and stands with us when the way grows dark and dangerous (Ps. 23:4). Yes, our Savior and Lord has been exalted in glory, but at the same time He stands with us as we do His will here on earth. Ponder Romans 8:31–39 and 1 John 4:4.

Jesus Holds Up and Builds Up

In this vast universe of which planet earth is a small part, what is holding everything together and keeping it on course? Scientists tell us that there are laws that govern these things, but where did these laws originate? According to John 1:1–3, Jesus Christ made everything; and according to Hebrews 1:3, Jesus Christ in heaven today is "upholding all things by the word of His power." The Greek word translated "upholding" means that Jesus is holding everything up, keeping everything together, and moving all things to fulfill their purposes and their assigned goals. Enthroned in heaven today, Jesus sustains everything by His word so that all things fulfill the will of God. If that were not true, Romans 8:28 could not be in the Bible; and that same word that sustains the universe should be allowed to sustain our lives and ministries.

Jesus is not only sustaining but He is also building. Before He entered into His public ministry, Jesus was a carpenter (Mark 6:3), which means He helped to build and repair houses, furniture, tools, wagons, and household items. Jesus built the universe and today He is building His church (Matt. 16:18; 1 Cor. 3:9–17; Eph. 2:19–22; 1 Peter 2:4–6), and each believer has a ministry to fulfill. The Lord also wants to build us up as His servants so that we are equipped to do His work for His glory. "And now brethren," said Paul, "I commend you to God and to the word of His grace, which is able to build you up and give you an inheritance among all those who are sanctified" (Acts 20:32). You find the word "edify" in some translations of the Bible, and it simply means "to build up" (Eph. 4:7–16). God builds us spiritually so we can assist in the building of the church (Eph. 2:10). And keep in mind that Jesus is building a heavenly home for His people (John 14:1–6), and this is a great motivating force for living the Christian life and seeking to win the lost.

Jesus Is Opening and Closing Doors

Jesus told the believers in the church at Philadelphia that He alone could open and close doors (Rev. 3:7–8). In Scripture, an open door is a picture of opportunity for service (1 Cor.16:8–9; 2 Cor. 2:12; Col. 4:3; Acts 14:27). The church is here on earth to minister not only to God's family but also to witness to unsaved people who need to trust the Lord. Sometimes we wonder how to reach people who are behind closed doors, but God can help us do it. When Dr. Luke wrote the book of Acts, he could have given it the subtitle "The Book of the Open Doors." The Lord gave the church opened doors of witness to unsaved religious leaders, governors and kings, business people, and even people in prison! When Paul in his travels started to go in the wrong direction, the Lord slammed the door shut and re-directed him (Acts 16:6–10). If we pray for God to open doors but they stay closed, we must accept it as the Lord's will and wait until the right time arrives for an open door. We must never try to pry the doors open against His will because that only results in trouble.

Solomon wrote, "In everything there is a season, a time for every purpose under heaven" (Eccl. 3:1). Only when God's work is done in God's way for God's glory *in God's time* will we experience God's blessing. The British spiritual leader Evelyn Underhill wrote, "On every level of life, from housework to heights of prayer, in all judgments and efforts to get things done, hurry and impatience are sure marks of the amateur." Another spiritual leader, Oswald Chambers, wrote, "To 'wait on the Lord' and to 'rest in the Lord' is an indication of a healthy, holy faith, while impatience is an indication of an unhealthy, unholy unbelief." Whenever I start to get impatient and am tempted to rush ahead and do things my way, the Lord often reminds me of Psalm 32:8–9. I recommend this remedy to you if you are in the habit of ignoring open doors and missing opportunities to share the gospel.

Jesus Is Watching and Waiting

I heard about a young Christian who was praising the Lord in a church prayer meeting for a blessing he had experienced, and he became so excited he said, "Oh, Lord, You should have been there!" But the Lord *was* there! In years past, my wife and I traveled a great deal in ministry and were always grateful for Psalm 91:11, "For He shall give His angels charge over you to keep you in all your ways." Whether on the highway, in the air, or just waiting, we knew that our loving Father was watching over us—and still is watching over us as we must stay home.

That the Lord is watching over His children ought to encourage us and not frighten us. For one thing, He knows when danger and temptation are near and can guide us to safety and to victory. As long as our motives are pure and our desire is to do God's will, we can count on His help; but if we have our own hidden agenda, the Lord first must deal with us. To deliberately want our own way is to tempt God, and to tempt God is to invite discipline. God watches over us for our own good, just as parents watch over their children. We learn from both victories and defeats, but the fewer the defeats, the better our spiritual education. God also has His eyes upon the nations (Ps. 66:7) and knows what they are saying, doing, and plotting (Ps. 2).The nations may rage against God and His people, but the Lord is not disturbed nor should we be.

Referring back to Psalm 110:1, Hebrews 10:13 tells us that Jesus is not only watching but also *waiting*. The word is sometimes translated "expecting," which means "ready to meet any situation." God is not in a hurry. He made the universe in six days but He took centuries to build the nation of Israel and to reveal His prophetic plan before He sent the Messiah. We don't know when Jesus is coming again and it's futile (and embarrassing) to set dates. The important thing is to be ready and not to be distracted by the world, the flesh, and the devil (Luke 21:34–36).

Have you ever noticed that each chapter in Paul's first epistle to the Thessalonian church ends with a reference to our Lord's return and gives the marks of those believers who are ready and eager to meet Him? If we are eagerly expecting our Lord's return, we will be:

1:8–10: witnessing and serving the Lord;
   2:19–20: hopeful and joyful;
      3:11–13: loving and growing in holiness;
   4:13–18: comforted in our sorrows; and
5:23–28: enjoying peace, purity, and prayer.

The blessed hope of our Lord's return should give us the assurance, encouragement, and joy we need in the midst of our trials and temptations in "this present evil age" (Gal. 1:4). I like the words of Charles Haddon Spurgeon, "I have a great need for Christ; I have a great Christ for my need."

And we do, too!

(*The Milestone Mirror: A Pause for Reflection*)

Your Savior is interceding for you in heaven (John 17:20; Rom. 8:34; Heb. 7:25). Do you take advantage of your fellowship with Him? Do you intercede faithfully for others?

When you confront problems and dangers in the will of God, do you look to your faithful High Priest to see you through? Ponder Hebrews 4:14–16.

Jesus is building His church and has given His people spiritual gifts to use in this construction project. Have you identified your gift(s) and are you using your gift(s) to help build the church? By your example and your words, do you encourage the other workers?

Are you making progress in discerning the will of God?

12

The Sending of the Holy Spirit

Acts 1–2

Our Lord had finished His earthly ministry, but there was one more milestone yet to be erected: the sending of the Holy Spirit to dwell in the believers. "Behold, I send the Promise of My Father upon you; but tarry in the city of Jerusalem until you are endued with power from on high" (Luke 24:49). By His example and His teaching, Jesus had already prepared His disciples for their future service; and now He would equip them further by filling them with the Holy Spirit. The Holy Spirit would enable the believers to carry on Christ's ministry and glorify God. "But you shall receive power when the Holy Spirit shall come upon you; and you shall be witnesses to Me both in Jerusalem, and in all Judea and Samaria, and to the end of the earth" (Acts 1:8).

One of the most important biblical images of the Holy Spirit is the special anointing oil described in Exodus 30:22–33. It was used only to consecrate prophets, priests, and kings *and to anoint people who had been healed of their leprosy* (Lev. 14:1–32). The priest first put the blood of a sacrifice on the person's great toe of the right foot, the right thumb, and the right ear; and then the priest *put the oil on the blood*. The priest would not put the sacred oil directly on human flesh, for the law demanded that the oil be placed on the blood. This procedure ties in with John 7:37–39, for Jesus had to shed His blood and be glorified before the Holy Spirit could be given to His people. In His upper room discourse, Jesus assured His disciples that He would not leave them orphans but would send the Holy Spirit to dwell in them and work in them and through them (John 14:15–18; 15:26–27; 16:5–15).

In the original Greek text, the word used for the Holy Spirit is *paracletos*, which is translated differently in various versions of the Bible: Paraclete, Comforter, Helper, Advocate, and Counselor. The Greek word means "one called alongside to help," for the Holy Spirit does God's work through us as we surrender to Him. The Holy Spirit is God's gift to believers (1 Thess. 4:8; Titus 3:5; 1 John 4:13) for their enlightenment, enablement, and encouragement. To be "filled with the Spirit"—a phrase used ten times in the book of Acts—means to be controlled by the Spirit. When people are filled with anger, or filled with grief, they are controlled by anger or grief. The first Christians spent ten days in prayer, preparing themselves for the coming of the Spirit (Acts 1); and when He came, He gave the church three wonderful privileges.

The Privilege of Being Receivers

Christians are receivers, not manufacturers. From the moment of our conversion to the instant we have glorified bodies, we depend on the Lord to give us what He has promised. We do not "manufacture" our ministry; we receive the dynamics and the directions from the Lord. God's people must wait on the Lord until He opens their eyes, opens the way, and empowers them for service. The first church tarried in prayer for ten days, knowing that God would keep His promise and send the Holy Spirit. Do churches today have prayer meetings? Do God's people today set aside time for prayer and wait on the Lord to send His blessing? I fear we are so busy manufacturing counterfeit "oil" (based on the world's formula) that we miss the blessing of the Lord completely. "If God were to take the Holy Spirit out of this world," said Dr. A. W. Tozer, "most of what the church is doing today would go right on, and nobody would know the difference." Like Nadab and Abihu, we bring false fire into the sanctuary instead of receiving the holy fire from heaven (Lev. 9:22–10:7).

It is a privilege to minister for our Lord, but we cannot do it in our own strength. "But you shall receive power when the Holy Spirit has come upon you," Jesus promised them (Acts 1:8), and they believed His promise. Before the believers could be involved in public ministry, they needed to be controlled by the Spirit of God, even as Jesus was as He ministered (Luke 4:1, 14, 18). The early Christians knew that Jesus was filled with the Spirit and that they would be filled also (John 14:16–18). The Spirit had dwelt *with* them in the person of Christ and would soon dwell *in* them on the day of Pentecost (John 14:17).

The church cannot function effectively apart from the power of the Holy Spirit, which explains why there are fifty-six references to the Holy Spirit in the book of Acts. To begin with, the Holy Spirit *unifies the people of God*. It is the responsibility of every Christian to endeavor to maintain "the unity of the Spirit in the bond of peace" (see Eph. 4:1–6). When our Lord prayed that we might be one (John 17:11, 20–23), He was asking for a living *unity with diversity* and not a dull *uniformity*. The Spirit was not sent to make us "cookie-cutter Christians" but to provide the church with people having a variety of gifts that blend together to accomplish God's will and glorify His name. The Spirit enables the church to enjoy unity and diversity as well as spiritual maturity so that the body is strong and healthy. Dissention and division are to the body of Christ what a stroke is to the human body: the parts stop working together and there is inefficiency and paralysis.

The Holy Spirit *gives us assurance that we are God's children.* The enemy accuses us and tells us that we are not the children of God, but the Spirit assures us that we are. Ephesians 1:13 and 14 inform us that the Spirit has sealed us, and this seal is a guarantee (down-payment, assurance) that we belong to God and have a future in heaven. What the Spirit's ministry is to us today is but a foretaste of the blessings we will have forever in heaven. The Spirit also *gives us access to the Father* (Eph. 2:18; 3:12; Rom. 5:1–2) so that we can worship, fellowship, and pray. The Spirit *intercedes for us* (Rom. 8:26–27) and helps us know and do the will of God. He *teaches us the word of God* (John 14:26; 15:26; 16:12–15; 1 Cor. 2:13). It is a splendid thing to have a formal theological education, but my diploma is no assurance that I have learned the deep truths of Scripture. All the years I have been a Christian, I have rejoiced in comparing Scripture with Scripture and discovering the nourishment and wonderment of the word of God.

If we are walking in the Spirit and seeking to glorify Jesus, the Spirit *reminds us of what He has taught us and enables us to apply God's truth to our daily lives.* The Spirit has often reminded me of a promise or a warning in Scripture just when I needed help. "Your word is a lamp to my feet and a light to my path" (Ps. 119:105). A drunken driver going eighty miles an hour slammed into my car one evening and might have killed me were it not for the grace of God. Have you ever ridden to the hospital inside an ambulance while the siren is blaring and the attendants are doing all they can to keep you alive? One verse possessed my heart as I lay there and I quoted it over and over in my mind: "Great is the Lord, and greatly to be praised; and His greatness is unsearchable" (Ps. 145:1). The Spirit is the Great Encourager and He uses the Scriptures to quiet our hearts, increase our faith, and assure us that all is well. Sometimes the Spirit gives a precious promise to an entire Bible class or congregation. "Then the churches throughout all Judea, Galilee, and Samaria had peace and were edified. And walking in the fear of the Lord and in the comfort of the Holy Spirit, they were multiplied" (Acts 9:31).

As God's beloved children, we are receivers. "And my God shall supply all your need according to His riches in glory by Christ Jesus" (Phil. 4:19). How do we receive what we need? By asking in prayer and believing God's promises. Charles Haddon Spurgeon said to his pastoral students, "However, brethren, whether we like it or not, asking is the rule of the kingdom." James warns us, "Yet you do not have because you do not ask." It has been proved over and over again that when the children of God are doing the will of God for the glory of God, when they ask of God, He will provide what they need. We are receivers! "Ask and it will be given to you" (Matt. 7:7).

The Privilege of Being Transmitters

The blessings we receive from God must be shared with others, because God blesses us so that we might be a blessing in today's crumbling world. Yes, we are receivers, but "it is more blessed to give than to receive" (Acts 20:35). Christians are not reservoirs to be admired but springs of living water that bring encouragement and enablement to others today. God says to us today what He said to Abraham centuries ago, "I will bless you . . . and you shall be a blessing" (Gen. 12:2). One of the great joys of the Christian life is to be a transmitter and help others to become transmitters. Jesus said, "Assuredly, I say to you, inasmuch as you did it to one of the least of these my brethren, you did it to Me" (Matt. 25:40, 45). When we serve others, we are serving Jesus and glorifying Him.

The word translated "witnesses" in Acts 1:8 gives us the English word "martyr," and the word translated "power" gives us "dynamite." A martyr is a person who gives his or her life to bear witness to the truth. Laying down one's life for the Lord is the ultimate in bearing witness. But the power to be a witness for Christ comes from the Holy Spirit, not from good grades in evangelism classes or reading books on soul-winning. Classes and books are helpful and important but the Holy Spirit's power is essential, and we have it only when we are totally yielded to the Lord. No matter what tasks the Lord gives us, we must depend on the Holy Spirit to enable us to say and do the right things at the right time in the right way for the right purpose. The Spirit imparts to us the gifts we need for serving the Lord effectively, but we must be completely yielded to Christ and obey Him if we want the Spirit's blessing.

We must be like the apostle Peter who, when commanded by his opponents to keep quiet, replied, "Whether it is right in the sight of God to listen to you more than to God, you judge. For we cannot but speak the things which we have seen and heard" (Acts 4:19–20). Witnesses are Christians who walk with the Lord, learn from the Lord, and thus are empowered by the Spirit to share with others their personal experiences with the Lord. They are moved by an inner compulsion from the Spirit. Witnessing is not manufacturing clever religious sales talks, nor is it debating theology or arguing about churches. Witnessing is lovingly sharing with others what Christ has done for us and what He can do for them. It is sowing the seed of the word of God in the hearts of people and trusting the Holy Spirit to convict them and bring them to faith in the Savior (John 16:7–11). It is encouraging to remind ourselves that we are not alone in our witnessing, for one believer sows, another waters the seed with prayer, and the Lord gives the harvest (John 4:31–39). The harvest may not come immediately, but the Lord of the harvest knows what He is doing.

We must keep in mind that witnessing not only involves speaking the right words but also living a consistent Christian life that backs up what we say. It means sincerely loving the lost, praying for them, and not being ashamed of Christ or the gospel (Mark 8:38; Rom. 1:16). Witnessing is not turned on and off like a light switch but requires that we constantly let our light shine to glorify Jesus Christ (Matt. 5:16). Feet walking in God's will, hands doing God's work, and a face shining with God's glory (2 Cor. 3:18; Acts 6:15) are the marks of the real witness.

The Privilege of Being Trailblazers

Before our Lord's ascension, His disciples asked Him if He would now restore the Jewish kingdom (Acts 1:6); and the Master replied that they should not worry about such things but focus on what the Father wanted them to do now. "But you shall receive power when the Holy Spirit has come upon you; and you shall be witnesses to Me in Jerusalem and in all Judea and Samaria, and to the end of the earth" (Acts 1:8). God's people are to be courageous trailblazers and not comfortable settlers. They should not be yearning for the past but looking toward the future.

An elderly member of one of the churches I served said to me, "Pastor, no matter what they tell you, the good old days weren't that good!" Some churches think they are conservative when actually they are only preservative. Like the lazy servant in the parable, they have carefully guarded what God committed to them but have done nothing with it (Matt. 25:18). I have friends who want the Lord to restore the Puritan era, while others long for the days of Moody and Sankey. I have been blessed reading about those days, but to try to duplicate them today may not be God's will. This does not mean that we should abandon the past; it means we should remember that history is a rudder to guide us and not an anchor to hold us back. Our Youth for Christ slogan says it best: "Geared to the times, anchored to the Rock." To ignore the past is to silence one of our most important teachers, but to try to duplicate the past is to attempt the impossible. This little poem has helped me keep the old and new in proper focus:

> Methods are many, principles are few;
> Methods always change, principles never do.

New methods grow out of old methods, but the old proven principles must not be replaced, especially those taught in the Scriptures. Our modern methods of transportation and communication are far superior to what Paul, Augustine, and Moody had in "the good old days"; but there are no substitutes for the God-given principles that have stood the test of time. It is always the right time for believers to be burdened about the sins of the nation and the state of the church. It is always the right time for God's people to confess their sins and pray for spiritual awakening. Referring to obedience to God's inspired word, Jeremiah exhorted God's people, "Stand in the ways and see, and ask for the old paths, where the good way is, and walk in it; then you will find rest for your souls" (Jer. 6:16). But walking on the old paths does not prevent us from dreaming new dreams, having new visions, and experiencing new power. Someone has said that what some old-timers say about the good old days is a combination of a bad memory and a good imagination; and being an old-timer myself, I am inclined to agree with them.

In building the church, Jesus would do a new thing: He would unite diverse peoples into one "people of God," where there is "neither Jew nor Greek, there is neither slave nor free, there is neither male nor female; for you are all one in Christ Jesus" (Gal. 3:28). Jesus commissioned the church to go into every nation and preach the gospel (Matt. 28:18–20). He saved Saul of Tarsus and made him Paul the apostle to the Gentiles, and Paul devoted his life to evangelizing the Roman Empire and planting churches. When the believers in Jerusalem became too comfortable, the Lord sent persecution that scattered them like seed into other cities, and more churches were planted (Acts 8:1–8). The Lord sent His Holy Spirit to an upper room in Jerusalem and filled His people with wisdom and power, and they opened the doors and went out to spread the good news of the gospel to a lost world.

Today we are prone to close the doors and as a "spiritual elite" enjoy the fellowship inside while the people outside perish. We have mapped out the old trails and love to walk on them, but we desperately need to blaze new trails. We must grow in grace and knowledge and understand that "if anyone is in Christ, he is a new creation; old things have passed away; behold, all things have become new" (2 Cor. 5:17). How much is new in our witness? The book of Acts reveals that God sometimes does things suddenly and we must be prepared. The sound of the "wind" of the Holy Spirit suddenly was heard and the believers were filled with the Spirit (2:2).Suddenly a bright light shined from heaven and Saul of Tarsus was blinded and thrown to the ground (9:3; 22:6). Suddenly there was a great earthquake and the doors of the Philippian jail were opened (16:26) and the jailer and his family were saved. We do not like sudden interruptions from the Lord. We work too hard to prepare each Sunday service and we do not welcome interruptions.

It is a good thing when local churches send out missionaries, but it is also a good thing when every member of a local church *is* a missionary right in his or her own world. I have ministered the word of God in churches where, as you enter the building, you see a sign that reads ENTER TO WORSHIP, and when you leave the sanctuary, you meet a sign that says DEPART TO SERVE, or perhaps YOU ARE NOW ENTERING YOUR MISSION FIELD. It is the Holy Spirit who sends us forth with the gospel (Acts 13:4) and empowers us to tell people how to go to heaven.

We must never get so involved with the new challenges that we forget to minister to the people who have been believers for many years. Paul re-visited the churches he founded so he could make sure the people who believed at his first visit were growing and serving. Paul had taught them and they were supposed to teach others. *One of the greatest needs in our churches today is obedience to 2 Timothy 2:2:* "And the things that you have heard from me among many witnesses, commit these to faithful men who will be able to teach others also." Here are four generations of believers, all of them a blessing! One of the greatest joys of my ministry has been the privilege of mentoring Christians called to the ministry, and I am still involved with some young pastors who are a delight and a challenge to know.

Henry Martyn, the godly missionary to India and Persia, wrote, "The Spirit of Christ is the spirit of missions, and the nearer we get to Him the more intensely missionary we must become." It is not necessarily miraculous experiences that identify a Spirit-filled believer, but the manifestation of the fruit of the Spirit (Gal. 5:22–23) and the proclamation that Jesus is the Son of God and the savior of the world. The Spirit glorifies Jesus (John 16:14) and so does the Spirit-filled believer.

(*The Milestone Mirror: A Pause for Reflection*)

Your body is the temple of the Holy Spirit. Are you caring for it in such a way that it honors the Lord and enables you to serve Him effectively?

Your body is also God's "toolbox" for service. He wants you to use the various parts of your body as His tools to accomplish His purposes (Rom. 6:12–14). Dedicate to the Lord the body and the skills you have and seek to honor Him in everything. Ponder Romans 6:11–14. The Holy Spirit glorifies God as He enables us to do His will from a heart of love.

Stay on good terms with the Spirit! Do not grieve Him (Eph. 4:30) by deliberate disobedience or attempting to do things your own way. You will be robbing God of the glory that belongs only to Him. It is dangerous to lie to the Spirit by scheming to sin and trying to cover it up (Acts 5:1–11). A selfish attitude of repeated disobedience will quench the Spirit and rob you of the wisdom and power you need (1 Thess. 5:19). Willful resistance and rebellion to the will of God will only bring daily defeat, no matter how gifted we may be. The Holy Spirit is a trailblazer, using God's people to advance the cause of Christ. Are you forging ahead by faith or are you in a comfortable situation and unwilling to change? Our Master's call is, "Follow Me, and I will make you fishers of men" (Matt. 4:18–22). Do you believe Him? Will you follow Him?

The future is your friend when Jesus Christ is your Lord.